Moments at Marathon

Lyn Bodycoat

 A catalogue record for this book is available from the National Library of Australia

Copyright © 2019 Lyn Bodycoat
All rights reserved.
ISBN: 187692277X
ISBN-13: 9781876922771

Linellen Press
265 Boomerang Road
Oldbury, Western Australia
www.linellenpress.com.au

Acknowledgments

My sincere thanks go the following -
- Helen Iles - Publisher from Linellen Press WA
- The Society of Women Writers, WA
- The Carnamah Historical Society of Western Australia
- Greg Bodycoat - Researcher, advisor and editor
- Sandie Wallace - Researcher, advisor and editor
- Ruth White - Researcher
- Hazel Bothe – Researcher
- Lindsay Chappel – Researcher

and all members of my paternal family who supplied stories, information and who embraced the idea of creating a memoir with tremendous enthusiasm to preserve a period in history.

Contents

Acknowledgments iii
Contents v
Foreword vii
Chapter 1 - It's not about the gun 1
Chapter 2 - The Ugly Place 7
Chapter 3 - School Begins 13
Chapter 4 - Visitors Arrive 19
Chapter 5 - The Move to Marathon 26
Chapter 6 - Mum's life on the Farm 31
Chapter 7 - Fires Everywhere 37
Chapter 8 - Little Sisters 44
Chapter 9 - The Beginning of Bulk Handling 50
Chapter 10 - The Search in Belgium 55
Chapter 11 - Fast forward 100 years 61
Chapter 12 - A Bowling Green 65
Chapter 13 - An Adult World 71
Chapter 14 - Young Bill and Old Bill 76
Chapter 15 - Training for War 82
Chapter 16 - Going to War 86
Chapter 17 - The End is in Sight 94
Chapter 18 - Marathon – Here I Come 98
Epilogue 102
About the Author 106

Foreword

This is a coming-of-age story based on my father's memories, as told to me by Laurie himself during the writing of this book. I have therefore written it in his point of view.

Laurie Chappel arrived at Marathon Farm at the beginning of the Great Depression as a boy and returned from the Second World War as a man, ready to embrace challenges on the family farm at Winchester in the Northern Wheatbelt of Western Australia.

During the research for this book I have tried to capture farming life in the mid twentieth century. The stories capture an era of Western Australian history, with a sense of place and people around Marathon Farm near Winchester.

Lyn Bodycoat

Chapter 1

It's not about the gun

As Dad looked out the truck window he said "No Son. It's not about the gun" in response to my question about why we were going to live in Winchester. My parents had decided to buy this place, one hundred and eighty miles north of Perth, in Western Australia, when I had just turned eight, in 1929. I'd heard of Winchester rifles but to call a place after a rifle seemed a bit odd. When I questioned Dad, he told me Winchester was the name of a place in England and that was the likely reason for the naming of this tiny settlement. However, the notion of Winchester, in relation to rifles, was to play a major role in my later life. Dad had recently sold his farm in Victoria and I remember hearing the story of his brother who had bequeathed land to him when he died in the war. After a lot of deliberation, Mum and Dad prepared for a new life.

So began our sojourn across the Nullarbor with most of our belongings on the back of our truck, and what an adventure it was to become. Every night we erected our tents – kids in one and parents in another. Dad and I were on tent duty while Kitty helped Mum with dinner. While the bread and vegetables became increasingly stale, the meat was fresh as Dad shot a kangaroo or a rabbit almost every night and we cooked on a small kerosene cooker. Sometimes others joined us, but we were mainly on our own, so we entertained ourselves by watching the stars in the night-sky and telling stories. Breakfast consisted of eggs with bread, once again, and soon we would be on our way to endure mile after mile of flatness and tedious sitting in the truck, reading and playing cards. Day after day this continued until we neared Kalgoorlie, which was a great place to camp and explore. Even our parents were keen to spend some time in this historic town with its gold-mining history. The people panning for gold and digging with spades were everywhere and I was surprised at how intent they were on finding gold granules in their panning dishes while some just dug the ground with a crazy notion of making their fortune.

I was pleased we were going to spend a whole day and perhaps two nights here buying some supplies from bustling shops. I decided to get out my cricket bat, the stumps and ball to play a game.

"Kitty, you can bowl, and I'll bat," I called to her as I used the sledge hammer to bang the stumps into the hard, red dirt. This time we all decided a game would be a great idea.

"What about you Dad?" I called out between the hammer noises on the stumps and my efforts to chase the flies away from my face.

"Not this time, Son. I've got to go and see someone about something."

He was always going somewhere to see someone about something and when he did, it was usually to our benefit, so this was quite a familiar pattern for me.

"Where are you going?"

"There and back to see how far it is." That was what he always said.

Our game began in its normal pattern with Kitty pitching up to the leg side and I played a few defensive shots to get my eye in. Mum was watching in the shade but on alert in case I played one to the out-field. Soon a kid about my age came along and wanted to join in. I told him he was welcome to join in and find a spot in the field, which he did, but soon he wanted to bat.

"No, only Kitty and I get to bat."

He shouted angrily something about the rules, which I didn't understand, and soon he stormed off. Kitty and I swapped so that she got to bat and in a short time the same kid came back with his dad who demanded Alex had a turn at batting, so I was a little bit scared of this situation. I didn't have long to think about it because Dad came along with an armful of wood to make our camp-fire.

"Come along, Son. Game postponed now. We have work to do. What was going on?"

"This kid called Alex and his dad wanted to join in and change our rules."

"Who owns the equipment? Who is the captain? You own the equipment and you are the captain, so the rules are your rules and no-one else's."

Dad had spoken but it was a struggle for me because I thought Alex probably did have a point but there was no way I was going to verbalise my thoughts to Dad.

I didn't sleep easy that night and I couldn't stop thinking about Alex and his dad, who was well-built, with sweat making wet marks on his shirt. He looked intimidating – smoking his pipe and wearing a gentleman's hat – and I realised I was relieved when Dad had made his appearance. I listened to the night noises, and the sound of Dad snoring in the next tent reassured me that my world was okay and the next thing I knew it was morning.

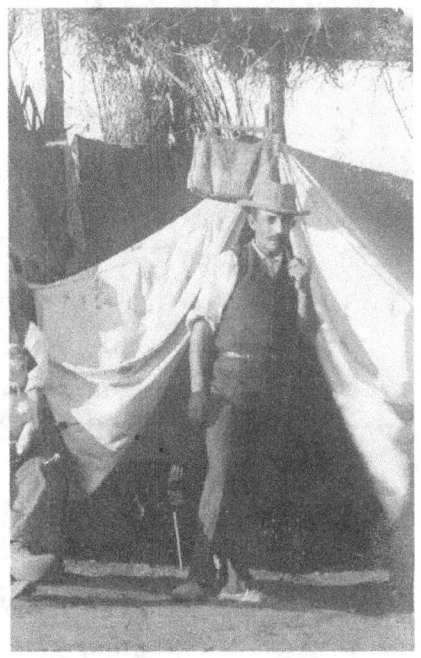

The sun was bright and the sounds of people moving as they went about their morning business filled the air, along with parrots making their own brand of noise in the trees. We packed some gear back into our truck and filled our water bags from a nearby tap in the camp site. A lady in the shop had told Dad about the famous waterpipe to Kalgoorlie all the way from the Mundaring Weir, wherever that was, but apparently the water to the goldfields was a landmark for the state of Western Australia and people were confident that Kalgoorlie would soon become more important than Perth. This confidence was founded by a gold discovery recently made not far from our campsite. I was later to learn about the Golden Eagle, the name of the largest nugget ever found up until now in this whole area. Anyway, men were in a frenzy and the excitement grew as each person thought that they could be the next person to find a Golden Eagle.

I was amazed to see men with their picks and shovels digging away in the dirt and the dust, with flies and the sun working as their nemesis. They had wheelbarrows with their tools, which they pushed around in their bid to dig here and there. Of course, I wanted to do some digging too so Dad took us off for a while so we could try our luck at making our fortune. I saw Alex along the way and told him we were going to make our fortune with some digging.

"Do you want to see some gold?" he asked me quietly.

My eyes grew as big as Mum's saucepans and I immediately wanted to see what he had found.

"Just walk past my tent in a few minutes when you can sneak back to the camp."

He was trying to make amends for his dad's anger and I was keen to correct an unfair situation, so I did what he said. Of course, I wanted to see some gold. I could hardly believe my luck as he furtively lifted the tent flap and invited me in. His parents were nowhere around so I felt quite relieved as he led me to a bucket of dirt near the back of his tent, where it was very dark.

"See that glittering stuff in the dirt? That's gold. See those little grains or granules of shiny yellow bits? That's gold."

My heart was thumping with excitement as he swore me to

secrecy.

"I know my dad has been quietly showing a few people, so I wanted to show you too. We are going to have it weighed and recorded tomorrow so that it will be official. Between now and tomorrow we just must make sure that no-one steals it so soon it will be my job to mind the tent. My dad will be back later."

At the mention of his dad, I thought that I'd better make myself scarce as I didn't want to see his angry face again and incur his wrath a second time. I felt sure he had a very loud voice.

I scampered away quickly hoping not to encounter anyone coming into the tent. I pretended to go to the tap for a drink and rest my thumping heart. I had to make sure too, that my voice didn't quiver so I waited for some time to make my appearance in our tent.

"I thought you were with your father" said Mum as she packed our bread away into a box. It was lucky she had her head down packing away dishes.

No-one looked at me, so I had time to compose myself and I thought it best not to say anything until Dad came home.

"Dad, you know that kid Alex? Well, he showed me some gold they had found. They are going to register it tomorrow and get some money for it. How much will they get?"

"Not sure, Son. Don't say anything to anyone about it though. People out here can steal and then kill for gold. Not much of the law out here either. In the morning I suggest that you say goodbye to Alex and then we'll clear out. Just wait until his dad goes and then say your goodbyes."

The next morning, after checking for the absence of Alex's dad, I caught up with my new friend, who didn't seem to have a mum. I told him we hadn't found any gold but we were on our way to a place called Winchester, where we were going to set up a farm and become farmers, just like we had been in Victoria. We had planned to get an early start to make as much travel distance as we could before nightfall, so I had to get back and help Dad pack up the truck after dismantling our tents. This all took some time, so I scampered off quickly wishing Alex all the best in his gold adventures.

Dad was waiting for me. We loaded up and drove off through the potholes and dust, eating our sandwiches as we went. We were aware we had to conserve our food and water until the next town and Kitty and I felt excited in our bid for a new life.

"Winchester here we come," sang Dad as he drove along.

Chapter 2

The Ugly Place

It was a cold day when Dad drove through the gateway into his newly purchased farm of 700 acres. I will always remember the look of disappointment on Mum's face when she saw the tin shed, which was to be our home. As we pulled up close to two massive gum trees near the drive-way, she looked mortified. Screeching white cockatoos seemed to mock us with their raucousness and I wanted to throw stones at them.

The countryside was like the landscape we'd called home in Victoria with its big gumtrees and rich red dirt. I was excited about living near a railway line and couldn't wait to listen to the rattle of the trains and figure out what was in the wagons. Dad had visited the Department of Agriculture on a previous visit to investigate the best area and the one which had the most reliable rainfall for wheat-growing. They had advised him to buy in the Northern Wheatbelt, near Carnamah, so we arrived on a wet day in September of 1929. Dad was pleased because it was raining, and the green grass was thick and long all around the sheds and dilapidated house that was to become our home, albeit very briefly. Well, at least that's what we all thought, but one year slipped by and then another few years too.

"Bess, there's not much of a house here but we'll soon fix that. The shed is fine, but we'll get onto the house as soon as we can. There must be a builder in the nearest big town."

Our old Ford truck slowed to a standstill and we clambered out as soon as we could, my sister pushing and shoving like she normally did. Kitty was two years younger than me and we were often a great team, but Dad was my ally and we sided together regularly to achieve what it was that Dad wanted in this business of family dynamics. Sometimes I wasn't sure what Dad wanted but I worshipped him, and this was my initiation into men's business and all the complexities that went with it. This was our new adventure!

"Don't worry Bess. We'll build a house as soon as possible. That's the first thing we'll do. It's no good having a good farm, without a decent house. You wait and see. It'll be the best house you have ever seen" and I could see his mind working out a plan.

The idling of the truck continued, just humming in the background, while he and Mum sat looking at the old shed, which was to be our house for the next six years. Dad's reverie didn't last long as he soon bounced out of the truck and stretched his legs. Six weeks of living in tents across the Nullarbor, arriving at the unknown, took the sting out of Dad's step, but it was only temporary. Poor Mum sat in the truck, stunned. The tears in her eyes were battling to stay there and not run down her cheeks.

"Come on, Mum. It's an adventure," I called out to her to follow Dad's lead and jump down out of the truck.

"All that effort, for this," she said. "And what are we going to call this farm, Howard? I guess it has to have a name."

By this time, she was out of the truck and looking around at the red dirt and big gum trees – similar to the landscape we had left in Victoria. At Rochester, the trees were big too and the dirt was red. "What an endurance!" I could see she was totally wrecked.

"Why don't we call it The Ugly Place?" So, The Ugly Place it became, and it was very aptly named. I was hoping the most difficult part was behind us but, by the look on Mum's face, I wasn't so sure.

The next morning Dad was in action. I could see he was on an adrenalin rush and found this energy exciting. He took off quickly while Mum was still putting the breakfast items out in the shed. We would all have to get used to referring to it as the house. She was used to this level of energy and she was aware of her role in this adventure too. As for me, I just followed Dad and Kitty followed me, almost running to keep up.

"Laurie, you and Kitty gather some wood for the fire while I patch some of the holes in the shed."

Soon after our arrival, an Aboriginal man appeared and told Dad he was the working man on this farm. Dad was ecstatic as more hands meant quicker progress. It was quite a few weeks before Dad slowed down enough to ask the man where he lived.

"My name is Bill Cornish and I live up there beyond that gate in the bush."

Until now Dad had simply been calling him 'mate' in the same way as he called me 'Son'.

"I have a son and a wife up there in the house."

Dad promptly asked him to bring his son, who was the same age as me, to work with him the next day. He just stopped himself in time before he was tempted to ask him to bring his wife to work too. Dad's exuberance for work was contagious but old Bill and young Bill were keen to go shooting for kangaroo and I quickly realised this was necessary for survival. Each evening at sunset young Bill and I set out with our rifles and moved quietly towards the dense scrub, watching for movement. Birds often disturbed the wildlife and warned them of imminent danger, which our rifles represented. Most evenings we were successful, and we soon worked out that we would only go shooting when it was necessary.

I showed Bill how to organise a hessian bag and let the water drip through to keep the meat cool.

"It's called a Coolgardie Safe, Bill. Haven't you heard of this?" Of course, he hadn't.

Soon, I realised that being a good shot with a rifle was highly regarded. We compared our rifles as Bill was a good shot too.

"Keep those rifles in a safe place, boys," said Dad, so we designed a section of the shed to accommodate rifles and bikes. Other parts of the shed were places for Dad's machinery and the sulky. A ride to church on Sundays in the sulky was an outing we all loved.

Dad's tractor from Victoria had arrived by train and he was keen to ensure that it was looked after. It was his prize possession and I knew that he would be wanting to put a crop in as soon as it rained, so every morning he searched the sky as though intensive staring would actually produce rainfall. Dad also realised that he would need to ensure harmony on the domestic front, so constructing a rainwater tank was his next task. Running a pipe from the tank to the house was critical and our dam water was to suffice until it started to rain.

Young Bill and I both loved helping men in a man's world; we were farm workers now, not just kids, even though I was just nine. This freed Dad up so that he could focus on farm business and it wasn't long before he was making unknown trips to unknown places for unknown reasons. I shouldn't say that really because soon some sheep and cattle were in our paddocks grazing on the grass.

"Dad, that's amazing!" Mum called him the miracle maker and I was lucky to grow up with parents who adored each other, regularly calling each other Mummy and Daddy.

Old Bill and Dad constructed the yards for the animals and soon a cow was in calf, which later meant milk and cream. Mum gave the cow a name – Daisy – and she knew how to milk it and how to make cream. Her next challenge was to make butter from the cream, and she looked forward to every challenge each day presented.

Poor Kitty had been relegated to kitchen-work, but we were aware that someone had to help Mum make food and carry buckets of water from the dam or the tank so that we had a continuous supply of water to boil. If the water wasn't boiled, then who knew what bugs were concealed beneath the surface. Once The Ugly Place resembled a house – now only just better than a tent – the rainwater tank would be connected for our fresh water supply. Dad really wanted his new farm project to work and it was critical to keep Mum happy. She was a champion really, because her life in Victoria was so much easier than her early days in Winchester. She had a really nice house in Victoria but Dad was keen to grow grain and wasn't so keen on irrigation and orchards. Mum had a brother, John Lampard, who was older and lived nearby, and he had been keen for us to move here. We saw a lot of Uncle John and Aunty May, along with cousins Agnes and Ben. Mum's sister, Aunty Mary, lived in Carnamah, and we instantly became friends with the Baker family. Regularly we would drive up Bakers Hill for an evening of fun and entertainment. Kitty and Dorothy often put on concerts while Phil and I were the audience and had to clap loudly and pretend we enjoyed it. Having a family so close was fabulous.

Soon it was Christmas and I still hadn't seen Mrs Cornish. "Mum, why doesn't she come down here?"

"I guess she wants to keep to herself, Laurie. Lots of people like their privacy and we have to respect that."

By this stage young Bill and I were becoming firm friends, but I knew he liked to spend time away from us with his family. They weren't really interested in Christmas but for me it meant a present and sure enough Dad had a surprise for us on Christmas morning. It was a dog: a black male kelpie came to join us at The Ugly Place and we were absolutely thrilled. I'm not sure where it came from, but there he was on Christmas morning with his tongue hanging out and his tail wagging furiously. He was called Darkie because of his black, shiny, furry coat and we loved him, taking it in turns to feed him each night, knowing that dogs love anyone who feeds them. Kitty had managed to lure a feral cat from the bush with titbits of food each night and now it was becoming quite tame. Rat-tail, as I nicknamed the cat, and Darkie quickly accepted each other but I could never say they were friends.

Chapter 3

School Begins

My happiness at working alongside Dad, with old Bill and young Bill, was soon interrupted when, after Christmas, Dad made a statement regarding school. He was never tactful about what was to happen, so Kitty and I had to prepare for this intrusion into our lives. Each day Mum prepared us for school in Winchester and drove us there and then home again in the truck. This was to continue for years. It seemed long and tedious, particularly in summer when I knew Dad needed me for harvest.

One day there was a lot of excitement at our school when a new teacher was about to start. As we were a one-teacher school, this meant a total staff change. Her name was Miss Robertson. Kitty really liked her. I was quite indifferent about who was teaching us. I just knew there was a class full of little kids and big kids who all did as they were told. Miss Robertson started in 1933, when I was one of the big kids. She left in 1936 and so did I.

About 1933

My main memories of school were recess and lunch-times when my friend Jack and I played cricket and football in the playground for as long as we could. We were always late back into class but Miss Robertson didn't seem to mind.

"Laurie, you can help James with his maths work and Jack you can help your sister."

I figured I got the best deal as James – or Jim as I called him – and I were good friends. Jim and I slowly built up a collection of marbles and on wet days we were allowed to play marbles with the other kids who were quite a bit younger than us. This was a game where girls could play too but the rule was that no-one was able to cry when they lost.

As a treat, I was able to ride my horse to school, as did quite a few other kids. One day, my poor horse was exhausted as we had spent the weekend on the fabulous Winchester Dingo Hunt where all riders, men, women and kids, were invited to hunt this dingo which had been seen lurking around our chicken yard.

We all met at our place early on a Saturday morning in the summer when the sun was warm, but the wind was cool. Mum had set up a trestle on the verandah and many of the ladies from the district arrived with scones and tomato sandwiches for morning tea. The wood stove in the kitchen was hot and boiling water for tea was plentiful. Kitty had to bring out all our cups and saucers, mindful that the chipped ones stayed in the cupboard. They were strictly for home use.

My job was to ensure the horses were looked after near the cow shed, making sure they had hay and water when they were in the yard securely locked up. When Jim's parents arrived, I called out to him to join me in the cow yard so he could help me with the horses.

"I'm going up to the house to wait for Jack and then we can get our own horses ready for some serious riding. I remember reading about a fox hunt and this is going to be a great day."

I could hear the excitement in my voice and my face registered the happiness I was feeling inside. I didn't care about the wind dropping and the temperature climbing. I just wanted the hunt to begin, but I was wise enough to realise kids rode at the back so they didn't get in the way. This was serious men's business. I just knew the dingo was going to 'get it' by the end of the day and I was glad I wasn't the dingo. I'm sure even the chickens knew they were about to gain a reprieve from a dingo's hungry gaze and the ewes and lambs would feel safer too.

Suddenly a shotgun sounded. This was the signal I'd been waiting for. "Quick, Jim, hurry up, put your saddle on and tie the girth real tight. We're not telling anyone what we're doing. We're looking after horses and that means we could ride them."

Jack was already out of the yard with his eyes on the riders, so he knew where they were planning to go. He wasn't as keen on justifying his actions as I was. I knew which gates were open and where the ride would begin so, to keep out of sight, we rode just past the house and towards the eastern paddocks. I pulled on the reins to stop Blackie from pig-rooting, but she could feel the excitement and could see other horses in the distance. She neighed and snorted as she threw her head backwards moving towards the gate. I pulled tight on the reins and she reluctantly obeyed her master, but I could tell she wanted to be part of the pack ahead.

The hunters on their horses galloped as fast as they could, and dogs ran with them. It really was like a fox hunt and, although my old horse Blackie and I wanted to be part of the action, I didn't want to incur Dad's wrath by getting in the way.

The dust was rising as they raced along, and it was getting into our eyes, making them water as we attempted to correct our vision and look for a dingo. I wanted to yell out to Jim and Jack in our excitement but the noise of barking dogs filled the air. I yelled anyway but I knew my voice would be lost in the turmoil. There was far too much anticipation looking for the dingo. I was oblivious of anything except hanging on and I let Blackie take her lead, with loosened reins and the noise of heaving horses filling my ears.

The second gate was approaching as men and beasts took their turn in moving towards the open paddock. The squeeze for space was on and I was keen to take control of Blackie so we could hide in the floating dust. Jim and Jack were nowhere to be seen and I had completely forgotten about them at this stage, knowing they were a long way back. Blackie didn't like the idea of slowing down and I pulled tight on the reins, creating a lot of discomfort for her. The next minute she reared up as the tight reins met with resistance and I fell backwards. The saddle slipped around and soon I was on the ground. I landed on my arm which I had tried to use to cushion my fall.

When I opened my eyes Jim and Jack were peering over me with worry written all over their faces.

"Did Dad see us?" That was my main concern and I didn't care less about my arm which wouldn't move, because of the pain.

"No. They've all raced ahead."

The noise and dust hung in the air while the sun beat onto us and we knew that our plan had gone wrong. We were meant to be looking after the horses, but I couldn't even see Blackie, knowing that she would be galloping towards the pack and soon Dad would see a riderless horse. This was never a good sign and my heart was racing. I could hardly stand up with fear and my arm wouldn't move.

"Hell, Laurie! What are we going to do? Let's wait for a bit while we plan. Let's not rush into this."

That was the summer I broke my arm and Dad still made me ride to school. It hurt like crazy but the shame of falling off a horse was greater than the physical pain in my arm. I just rode slowly and even Blackie knew we were in trouble. I think everyone felt sorry for me as I could feel my normal exuberance diminishing both in and out of the classroom.

I knew I had a bit more time before I could leave school so I had to lie low for a bit and not playing sport at lunchtime and recess proved very difficult. I had to stay inside and read- an activity that I quite liked doing, nonetheless. Dad eventually came to terms with my antics.

Chapter 4

Visitors Arrive

Kitty and I loved sleeping in the tents outside the house; it was our place of sanctuary where we owned our own souls and shared lots of thoughts. One day Mum told us there would soon be a new little baby arriving, so we thought that he or she might sleep in our tents.

"Mum, can it sleep in my tent?" asked Kitty.

Mum quickly quashed this idea as Darkie slept in my tent and Rat-Tail slept in Kitty's. She told us the new baby would be sleeping in the house. Mum was very wise justifying the arrival of a baby and where it was going to sleep. Anyway, we had to wait ages for the baby to arrive and Mum mentioned something about birds and bees but no way could I see a connection. That's what I loved about Mum – she was quick witted and the master of understatement. However, I didn't always understand what she was talking about. What I didn't like about her though, was she called me 'Lolly'. What a sissy name and now that I was becoming a big kid, I didn't like it. Oh well, a new baby was coming sometime in the future. I was hoping it would be a boy but it turned out to be a girl, whose name was Hazel.

Some visitors, who weren't as welcome, were the boy Alex and his father, who we had met on the goldfields. Dad and I had been working at the shed when, above our noise, I heard the sound of an approaching vehicle. I peeped out of the shed to see an old truck slowly rumbling up the drive, splashing mud out of the puddles and making our track to the main road even more treacherous than ever.

The cockies screeched out loudly as the truck noise disturbed their morning chewing of the gum leaves and they all flew out of the trees, as if they anticipated tension. I had never really liked the look of Alex's dad and, as they both became visible through the windscreen, the hair on my neck started bristling as I looked into their eyes. It was good to see Alex, but my fear of his dad left my legs quivering.

"Where's your father?" called out Alex's dad as he alighted from his truck and strode towards our shed.

I didn't quite know what to say but I think I must have looked in Dad's directions. Once again Dad saved the day as he could hear hostility in the man's voice. "Let's go to the house for lunch and our visitors can join us."

We all sat around the table and before Mum served us our usual cold meat and salad, Dad spoke. "So how can we help you?" with a formal tone that was quite unusual for him. Alex had said nothing. I hadn't spoken either. This seemed like men's business.

"When your boy Laurie was in our tent in Kalgoorlie, he took some of our gold!"

"Is this correct, Laurie?"

"Of course not, Dad!"

"Alex, I think you and your father had better leave after lunch."

"I'm not going until I have my gold."

War had been declared and my heart pounded in my chest so loudly that I was sure others could hear it, but I didn't care. I kept looking at the cold mutton and the slice of tomato on my plate. There were some little flowers painted on the edge of the plate and I made my eyes focus on them.

"Bess," Dad called out with authority and when Mum entered the room, he looked at her. "Go and get old Bill and young Bill. Tell them to come here immediately. Then ensure the truck is ready to drive to town."

Seconds crept on and when I saw Dad eating his lunch, I

assumed the same action. Tension hung in the air, and no-one said anything. My heart continued its pounding as I lifted my fork to my mouth. Kitty followed my actions. I could even hear Darkie panting under my chair as he flicked his head from side to side.

Old Bill and young Bill rushed inside letting the fly-wire door bang loudly. "What's up Boss?"

Dad motioned them both to stand at his side while he remained motionless in the chair.

"Bill, these men are just leaving."

Silence filled up those empty spaces again. The seconds dragged past like years.

"Bess, I want you to drive into town and bring out the police immediately. These men are trespassing."

With her head down, Mum quietly left the room, taking her apron off as she moved towards the door. As she quietly hovered near the pantry, Alex's dad rose to his feet pushing his chair back as he did so.

"I don't think it will be necessary. Come on, Alex" he muttered quietly, keeping his head down. As he slunk out through the door, he lifted his head and looked Dad square in the eyes and said clearly, "I don't think we are wanted here."

Dad maintained his gaze and said nothing.

We listened as their truck engine started and the gears clicked into place. Slowly the idling ceased as the throttle was engaged and the humming of the engine began. We could hear it turn around and gradually increase its pace down through the puddles towards the main gate. We were all very good at recognising an engine's progression. Soon it moved onto the main road, increased its pace and eventually the noise became silence. We all sat there stunned. Even Mum knew better than to say anything.

"Righto you two Bills! We have work to do."

Only that night, sitting at the table, was I brave enough to embark on a conversation. "Dad, were you scared today?"

"One is often frightened in the face of adversity but the idea of standing up to bullies is important. I thought about having young Bill on stand-by with the Winchester cupboard unlocked. But, Laurie, they were only small-time thugs trying to flex muscle. They weren't really criminals, but I don't like the example the old man is setting for his son. Poor Alex – with a father like that."

I couldn't get the thoughts out of my head and the following day I verbalised these thoughts. "Dad, would they know about a Winchester cupboard?"

"Yes, Son, but rifles are used for hunting only. Perhaps in an emergency, as a deterrent. Anyway, let's talk about something else." Dad, in his gruff kind of way, was good at ending conversations and we were all content to change the subject into something more pleasant.

Soon it was time to return to the shed. Kitty was left to help Mum clean up and attend to the baby while I had the excuse of attending to men's business until the end of the day.

"Kitty, come and look here," I called out to her as she emptied the teapot into the outside drain after breakfast the next morning. I bent down to peep through a nail hole in the corrugated iron wall of the wash-house, arching my back into position as I did so. I could hear someone coming along the track, pushing a bike and puffing at the same time. The swishing of a woman's skirt let me know the visitor was female, so I looked hard to determine her identity through the tiny circular hole.

"What are you looking at?" whispered Kitty as she clamoured towards her peeping hole in the wall. "Oh, that's Miss Robertson. I wonder what she wants? If we listen carefully, we may hear, so keep quiet, Laurie."

Miss Robertson was our teacher and I was sure she only had bad things to report on me. I listened with great trepidation as my heart rate increased.

"Oh no. I wonder what she's going to say?" I whispered as Mum came out wiping her hands on her apron, greeting the visitor warmly. They both went into the kitchen so Kitty and I soon aborted our listening mission and strolled down to the shed with Darkie closely following.

Soon after dinner Mum revealed the purpose of Miss Robertson's visit and I was so pleased that school wasn't mentioned. She prattled on about how Miss Roberson was boarding with Clyde and Rita Haig. I chuckled when Mum said that the Haig kids, Brian and Margot, had to refer to Miss Robertson as Aunty, when they were at home and then they had to call her by her school name whilst at school. I guessed it seemed fair. The letter Miss Robertson delivered was from Grandma, and later Mum read the letter aloud to us.

"*My dear Bess and Howard,*

I do hope this letter finds you all well and hopefully the children are well too. I am delighted to inform you that I will be visiting soon and will travel by boat from Victoria to Fremantle. I considered using the train, but I think the sea air will be beneficial to my health. I have been feeling out of sorts lately so this decision was one that I seriously considered. Papa has also been unwell so we will await his recovery. I will enclose a photo of him tending to his vegetable garden. The carrots have been particularly plentiful this season. Can you remember this tree? It is the one you used to climb when you were little.

Did the train suit the transport of the tractor when you left Victoria? I think you were so brave to transport your lovely Studebaker car too. To think they both arrived in Winchester and then you were able to unload them from the siding with the use of a ramp! I am so looking forward to seeing your farm and your town where the children go to school as well as where you buy your stores. I look forward to meeting your neighbours and of course, our lovely family, the Bakers and the Lampards. I miss all my dear children, Bess, despite you all being mature adults.

I was distressed to read in your last letter about the recent floods in poor Winchester and the store owners, the Mulligans, must have lost a lot of stock. Did the community rally around to help them? Howard, you are so civic minded I'm sure you helped as much as you could. Gosh all the water! And who are those people on the verandah?

It is time for me to conclude my letter now to my precious family, and it fills me with joy knowing I will see you all soon. I will write again soon with details of my arrival at Fremantle. Shall I catch the train to Winchester or will you pick me up in Fremantle? I await your response, dear Bess.

Your ever loving Mother"

I was excited about their imminent arrival and began all sorts of activities to make their stay enjoyable. Papa was an excellent shot with a rifle, so I planned to improve my skills to impress him.

∽❦

Chapter 5

The Move to Marathon

By the time Grandma and Papa arrived in 1936, we had moved to Marathon, which was an adjoining farm purchased from Mr Albert Cousins. Prior to that it had belonged to Mr Arthur White. This was 1000 acres so now the family farm consisted of 1700 acres. We called it *Marathon* for many reasons.

This was a great year with moving to a new house and enjoying my friendship with young Bill. I was keen to practise my rifle shooting and target practice to try to beat young Bill as we were both very competitive. It was also necessary as shooting birds needed to happen daily to feed Rat-Tail and Darkie who were both good at chewing through feathers and devouring the part of the bird that nourished them.

"Bill, guess what?" I was keen to count down the days until Papa's arrival and then show him around the farm. I wanted Bill to be part of the action too. "My grandparents are coming to stay."

Bill was totally ambivalent about grandparents, but our family regularly referred to the importance of family. In my head I was thankful to Arthur White for building this house on the new farm as now I could move into a bedroom, not that I minded sleeping in the tent – it was fun.

As I wandered along the verandah ready for morning tea, the smell of baking buns wafted out from the kitchen and this made my stomach rumble. Mum was a master of yeast buns and had won prizes in the Carnamah Show for her cooking. I quickly ran through the fly-wire door, letting it bang in the process, and sat down ready to consume some yummy food; my mouth watered with the thought. She had also won prizes for cream puffs, sponge cakes and fruit cake but today I was only concerned with the familiar smell of yeast buns that filled our new house.

As I looked across at Mum at the table, I could tell she was in one of her thinking moods and I assumed she was planning for the family visitors.

Mum wasn't sure where her parents were going to sleep in the new house and, despite some warm weather in recent times, April could still have cold nights. They would have to sleep in our bedroom so the tents would need to come out again. We loved this idea as being part of the outdoors and star gazing long after dark suited us.

Often Mum and Dad could hear us talking but they ignored this and just hoped we weren't too tired for school the next day. The years had slipped past but now Mum was conscious that a visit from her parents would be inspectorial. She needn't have worried, however, as our grandparents were only too happy to relax when Dad picked them up from the Winchester siding on a beautiful autumn day. Their ship had sailed into Fremantle and they had to catch the train to Midland and then the passenger train to Winchester.

The railways had been an integral part of early settlement and, being short of money, the government of the day had called for investors. These investors were mainly from England. The agreement was that for each mile of track laid, the company received twelve thousand acres of land, to be within forty miles of the line. This could be sold to local farmers or settlers. Laying of the tracks commenced at both ends, Midland (near Perth) and Walkaway (near Geraldton), and joined up in the middle near Carnamah. This was finally finished in 1894. Each week, freight and passengers utilised the railways, and this proved to be totally essential for success in the northern wheatbelt. Now, in 1936, our elderly grandparents arrived, exhausted but eager to visit their West Australian children.

Papa's favourite game was chasing little Hazel around in the lounge room. He would also make out he was a lion and hide behind the big flour bin, which stood three-foot-high. He would growl like a lion, trying to frighten us. I assumed this was how old people played with kids. Hazel enjoyed the game, Kitty allowed him to be indulged while I thought he was rather silly. My manners would never allow me to reveal my thoughts, however, so I simply indulged him too. I much preferred to be with Dad, doing men's business and trying to feel like a man instead of a kid. They stayed for a few weeks, then went to stay with the Bakers at Carnamah and with the Lampards at Waddi Forest.

Now that we lived at Marathon, we had to ride our bikes to school which was an activity I enjoyed. With the wind in my hair and the sun on my face, I could make up imaginary games where young Bill and I were chasing rebels of different kinds. Of course, Bill and I always won and by the time I arrived at school, my imaginary game finished, and we had to interact with other kids like Bruce Straiton and Keith Morrison, who was the son of the Winchester Store owners. Bruce was often absent because he had to help on the farm and I secretly wished I could be away and help on the farm. I later found out the reason Bruce had to help, was because his father had recently died.

One day as I was riding my bike to school I encountered Rex Solling's bull munching away, oblivious to all around him. I knew I shouldn't look an animal in the eye, so I just put my head down, pushed hard on the pedals and put up with the pain inflicted from my case banging on my legs. With a headwind blowing into my face and my heart pounding, I shouted out to Kitty behind me to hurry up.

This bull was still there when it was time to ride home and just when I was alongside the bull, the mud in my bike wheels clogged up and I fell off. The front wheel turned sideways as if it had a mind of its own. I grabbed hold of the handle bars and, with legs like jelly, pushed the bike along the muddy track thinking that I would dislodge the mud after I had escaped this bull.

When I was safely inside the gate, I removed the mud and burst into tears, mindful that I had just escaped the ferocity of that big, black bull. Mum reminded me that it was okay for big kids to cry but I asked her not to tell Dad – I wanted him to think I was brave. I found comfort in talking to Darkie and the other dogs and just hanging out at the shed around the machinery. I knew this was where I wanted to be.

Soon the day came when I turned fourteen and, at the end of the year, Dad let me leave school and help him permanently. Of course, this involved listening to Mum at the lunch table while Dad excused himself and had a sleep on the dining room floor. He called this his 'ten-minute siesta' and maintained that this allowed him to work better in the afternoon, but I wasn't convinced: I think he used this as his escape from the table. However, it was a small price to pay as listening to Mum talk wasn't very thrilling but, of course, I indulged her and listened attentively. At some stage, Mum became tired and joined Dad for a siesta. Soon it became a family ritual and then I joined them both.

Chapter 6

Mum's life on the Farm

Mum was pleased when I left school and she could hardly believe her little 'Lolly' had grown up.

"Bess, don't call him that," Dad reminded her as she put the meat pie into the oven of the wood stove. "He's a man now and he's wanted to be a man for so long. Let's be fair to him."

Of course, she loved her first-born, so she wanted to please me. Besides, she had Kitty and little Hazel, and even Hazel wasn't so little anymore. She comforted herself by thinking all mothers indulge their children and she was overwhelmed by recent news on the wireless about hardships of others in this Depression. She simply couldn't imagine other children not having enough to eat.

We had just come home from the Sunday School picnic where there was an abundance of food prepared by all the good cooks in the district. It had been at the nearby Yarra Yarra Lake where there had been fifty-five children.

"Bess, you did a good job of driving and making many trips in the car continuously for the day," said Dad and they reflected on the success of the afternoon.

Mum had made tomato sandwiches after baking her own bread and growing her tomatoes as well as making her favourite fruit cake. Others had made food too and she was mindful of the oranges grown on the farm being slightly dry. She must remember to water the tree more next year, but water was not to be wasted. It was such a dilemma. It had been a lovely September day in 1937 and the weather that year had been kind to farmers. It was spring and soon the harvest would begin. She needed to prepare for the hot times ahead.

As good Methodist churchgoers, Mum and Dad were aware of civic duties, as well as ensuring that their own family were not victims of the Depression.

"Bess, what do you think about the idea of building a tennis court?"

When this question was asked at the table clearly Mum wasn't the only person expected to give a response. I thought this was an excellent idea and so did Kitty. We shouted out and began an imaginary tennis game yelling out scores and trying to beat each other. We loved being competitive.

"Dad, we can do that before harvest!"

The tennis court idea gathered momentum. No sooner had the Sunday School picnic been held, when the tennis court project began.

"Bess, I told you we would have a decent house and now we're going to add a tennis court."

Mum was very excited and totally endorsed Dad's ideas. She remembered how she'd been attracted to him all those years ago when he visited Jeparit and they saw each other near Lake Hindmarsh – a fair bit different from Lake Yarra Yarra. She fell in love with his enthusiasm for new projects. Here he was again embarking on something no one else had even thought of. They had both been good sportspeople and this was a wonderful thing for the children, as well as themselves.

She set about clearing the table as everyone else had fled the scene to build a tennis court. "Oh yes," she said to Rat-Tail, "you'd better get used to avoiding tennis balls." She went outside and joined in serious discussions about the position of the tennis court.

Visitors were frequent. Often we knew them and sometimes we didn't. We were accustomed to salespeople knocking on the door, with their impoverished faces, desperate to make a sale. Whilst some were trying to sell their wares, others were trying to sell their labour. These visitors were becoming more frequent as the Depression of the 1930's continued to bite, so we tried to support everyone who had mouths to feed. We had taken on more workmen as, with the increased acreage at Marathon, we required more help than Bill and young Bill could provide. I was concerned that we had left Bill and young Bill at the Ugly Place.

"Mum, what will they do?"

Mum had to remind me about the vegetables they had grown, the way they could sell rabbits and vegetables to regular visitors, the hunting ability of both Bill and young Bill – not to mention they wanted to stay in their home – which was there before we arrived. They were keen to share so they would survive and they liked people coming to see their wares.

"Okay, Mum, I guess you're right." Mum had a way of making everything seem normal and I loved that about her.

She loved to cook and clean, but sewing was the thing she loved most and I admired the way she made clothes for Kitty and Hazel. One day a travelling sales person sold her some fabric and encouraged her to make a dress for herself.

"I'm not sure I can do this," I heard her saying to Dad late one night when we were supposed to be asleep in our tents.

"Of course you can, Bess."

With his encouragement she took to the fabric with the scissors the very next day after Dad and I had left for the shed. Soon there was an anxious call for Dad. This usually meant there was a snake or something similar, so I didn't take any notice. Mum's distressed face at morning tea told me something was wrong.

"Dad what happened?"

We were on our way back to the shed when Dad revealed the events of the morning.

"Your mum made a bit of a mess of her sewing, so I told her to wrap it all up and send it to Perth to a tailor. Can you deliver it to town later today? I have other things to send to Perth so it can go on the train tomorrow. Hopefully her dress will be back within a month." Dad and I shared a quick chuckle but this was serious business for Mum. Dad told me that her pride was not to be hurt so it was to be kept a secret.

I saddled up my horse soon after lunch and went to the shed for Dad's parcels but there was only one package for the mail. When I looked at Dad questioningly, he just winked. "Off you go," so off I went. It was only a few miles to the siding but the birds were particularly noisy that day so I made a mental note to go to Bill's camp later and shoot a few. I found their noise very annoying and while Mum complained about the flies, the bird noise drove me mad. One of the dogs had pups recently so there were more dogs to feed and that meant more dead birds which brought a smile to my face. I hated the way birds tore leaves off the trees and the poor trees were bereft of protective leaves so that sticks and twigs replaced greenery. My aim was to eradicate as many birds as possible and the more practice I had with the rifle, the better I was becoming. I was quickly on my way to young Bill's for bird hunting, with Mum's parcel on its way to the tailor.

Sometime later we prepared to go the Carnamah Show and I had forgotten the incident regarding the fabric and the tailor.

"Come on, you lot. It's time for a photo," and with that we were all outside posing for yet another one of Dad's photos.

"Laurie, you can take one of your mother and me."

I recognised the fabric and Mum's dress instantly. Dad's face was steel because he saw me looking quizzically, but I never said a word as I remembered what he said about pride.

"Mum, you look great!" and she did too.

Lyn Bodycoat

Chapter 7

Fires Everywhere

Mum won many prizes at the Show in Carnamah and she was quite proud of herself for her cooking prowess. Cream puffs, fruit cakes, plain cakes and white bread were some of her prize winners. She loved it too and Dad regularly complimented her on how she had settled into Winchester life after leaving Victoria.

While other members of the Mulligan family remained in the district, the farewell party Mum and Dad held for George and Esther Mulligan was a real credit to Mum, and the piano we had recently acquired was an enormous hit. It was a pianola and Dad had arranged for it to be railed to the Winchester siding just in time for the party. I drove the truck to the siding and then reversed up to the rail wagon for easy loading.

"You'll be getting your licence soon, Laurie. You've had enough practice. When we're loaded up, you can drive home."

There was a lot of singing that night and the Mulligans enjoyed a good send-off as they left the district for other adventures. I loved the singing but soon after, I was with Kevin and Jack, and we decided to try out the art of smoking.

The shearers had recently been to shear our sheep and one of them left some cigarettes and beer behind. We lads decided we'd give it a go at the next opportunity. We had arranged this at our weekly tennis matches at our house and that night was the night when we would be initiated into the smoking and drinking world of men. We were careful not to tell anyone, particularly little sisters, who were ready to reveal everything to our parents. They loved getting others into trouble, but they weren't going to get the opportunity with us that night.

We crept down to the shed thankful it was a moonlit night so easy access was assured. We snuck up the steps and into the darkness of the shed aware of the urine smell of penned sheep which hit us as soon as we entered. The bales were stacked up to the roof ready for loading, so we found a place next to them and put out three glasses so that we could have a drink of beer first. The initial sip was awful and I felt like spitting it out.

"Heck! Who could drink this?" Jack cried out while Kevin drank his and thought it was 'very tasty.' Jack and I decided he could finish off the bottle if he liked it that much, so he did. Jack and I waited patiently and marvelled at how he could like such a sour taste.

After what seemed an eternity, the bottle was empty, so Jack and I were keen to light up. We had watched how the shearers did it and it seemed easy enough. I had the cigarettes and Kevin had the matches, so it was time to share them around amidst the darkness and quietness in the shed. We each had a few matches to strike to ensure that we could puff away at a cigarette expecting a lovely sensation as that's what we'd seen with others. The next moment I felt a coughing fit come on and it felt like I was choking. I coughed harder and so did the others. We stood, stumbled and then collapsed feeling totally disappointed. Heaven help us, I thought. We must have somehow dropped our cigarettes as the next minute we could detect a smouldering odour from somewhere. We looked around and saw that one of our cigarettes had made contact with a bale and there was smoke drifting upwards from the floor.

"Crickey! Put out the fire!"

It wasn't really a fire at that stage, but Kevin was unable to move so we pushed him out of the way and felt around for a bag to put out the smoke. Of course, we couldn't see so we had to feel around for a bag terrified that at any moment we would see a flame. Jack found a bag first and hit the smoke continuously for several minutes until it went out. I lit a match to inspect the damage and found a hole in the bale and some of the wool had been burnt but at least the smoke had disappeared.

I heard a soft patter of footsteps come up the steps of the shearing shed and my heart froze! I couldn't see a thing but as I adjusted my eyes in the dull light and looked towards the door I whispered, "What's that noise?" to no-one in particular.

"It's a fairy," slurred Kevin as he slumped further alongside the bale of wool and promptly started snoring.

"It's a four-legged fairy with a furry, swishy tail and a slobbering tongue," replied Jack as Darkie came to towards us with his sharp toe nails tapping on the wooden floor. Soon he licked me and nestled in ready for a play. "Darkie, you scared us!"

Soon a two-legged silhouette appeared in the doorway. It was Kitty. "I knew if I followed Darkie, I'd find you. Mum wants you up at the house and needs you to bring in some wood for the fire in the lounge. Yuk! What's that smell? What have you lot been up to?"

"Never you mind," and with that I leapt up and ran from the shed, Darkie closely behind. "Darkie, you gave us away you naughty dog," but Darkie didn't care as he continued to walk in front of me, getting in the way. "Look out silly dog."

I reached the wood heap, picked up pieces of wood and entered the house as nonchalantly as I could whistling away to create a relaxed impression.

They were still gathered around the pianola singing to the tune of 'Galway Bay' so I joined in and sang loudly with gusto. Just casually, I asked Dad if a few of us lads could sleep in the shed and could he please ask Jack and Kevin's parents as well.

"Thanks, Dad," and with that I took off back to the shed. Unfortunately, Kitty was still hanging around. "We're going to sleep now, Kitty," I said as I threw some blankets at Kevin and Jack hoping she would leave.

The next morning, I woke up with old Bill standing over us holding a piece of string and a bag needle in his hand. "I guess you'd be needing this to do some repair work?"

What a genius that man was. I immediately got to work and sewed up the hole made by the cigarette the previous night.

"You lads are loading up those bales and I reckon it'd be a good idea to hide the burnt bag in the middle. The rail carriage is booked for late morning."

Soon we were all loading bales onto the truck, heaving and puffing, with sweat pouring off us. Poor Kevin looked pale but he never said a word as he rolled bales and heaved them onto the truck.

"Bill, can you tell Dad we'll take the truck to town to unload? Thanks man. I owe you."

Soon after this I went into the shearing shed to rescue cigarette packets and the beer bottle but they were gone.

"Bill, did you take away the cigarette packets and beer bottle?"

He shook his head and then I drew the dreadful conclusion that Dad must have. I couldn't meet his eye that night during dinner even when Mum asked how we liked our meat pie. I didn't feel hungry but I had to eat it all to keep up a front.

I kept a low profile for a few days and finally Dad suggested we do some fencing together down near the main road.

"Great idea, Dad," and we drove to the main gate to begin measuring and wire cutting. We heard a low humming noise as the day was hot and the sound travelled well.

"I'll bet that's Heinrich Bothe driving his car into Carnamah."

I looked into the distance and could make out two men sitting in the front of the car with MI-20 on the number plate. Yes, it was the Bothes. The dust blew around the sides of the car and the noise increased as Dad and I looked up from our wire cutting to watch, quite relieved for any distraction.

Suddenly, when the car was almost level with us, and we could see the men looking at us, it swerved to the right and rolled off the road and into the bush – it must have hit a pothole. It all happened so quickly. Soon the car was on fire as there must have been petrol leaking from a ruptured fuel line.

"Laurie, go and use the water bag to put out the fire and I'll get the truck."

My adrenalin kicked and I raced across the road and could see the two men had somehow been thrown into the back from the rolling force of the accident. I struggled to open the back doors and they managed to squeeze through twisted metal and started to extract themselves from the burning wreckage while I poured water and shovelled sand over the fire. Thankfully Dad turned up in the water truck, threw buckets of water on the wreckage and screamed for us to get away. I finished dragging them out, grabbed hold of the men's hands and we ran across the road and out of range of a possible explosion.

In absolute shock we watched as Dad attempted to put out the fire. Soon it was only a smoulder. No one spoke for what seemed ages. It could have been a disaster had the fire set alight all the crops in the district. I thought a catastrophe had narrowly been averted.

Even Kitty had the good sense not to question me when I slinked back into the house to recover. I heard Dad speaking on the phone and felt relieved that he had taken charge.

"Yes, this is Winchester three. Please organise for a truck to pick up a car wreckage just in front of the main gates at Marathon."

Our telephone had only recently been connected and to that point it had been used only for social occasions, such as organising sport. This time the telephone conversation was serious.

Some weeks later I wondered what happened to the two men; I assumed Dad must have taken them home. Kitty gave me such a stern look that I had to quietly admit I had learnt my lesson about fires. They were dangerous and were to be avoided as much as possible.

"Laurie, can you and young Bill get started on the fire breaks around all the paddocks and that should keep you busy for a while."

I thought he was going to say it would keep me out of mischief, but I think he allowed me to retain my dignity. He was just so wise!

Weeks later I drove past the garage in Coorow and tried to look for the car wreckage but it was nowhere to be seen. I was in the truck, too young to have a licence, so I thought I'd better keep my eyes on the road as I didn't want to end up like the Bothes.

Chapter 8

Little Sisters

Kitty and Hazel loved the tennis court and at one stage the kids were playing more than the adults. Mum and Dad were members of the Winchester Tennis Club but it was great when others came to our home to use the court. Kitty and I often played together, as well as against each other, and I felt that my love of sport came from the effort I put in.

When we put down the surface of the court with Colas (bitumen), it splattered black muck all over my legs because of my annoyance with the watering can which Dad had told me to use. It kept blocking and required cleaning. It took all day to empty out the 44-gallon drums and by late afternoon I'd had enough of trying to surface the tennis court. It had been hot and windless, and I could feel sweat running down my back. My tongue felt as dry as a cockie's cage in the desert, but I struggled until all the drums were empty, and the surface was smooth and even. Finally at sunset, I stood back to admire my work. It then occurred to me that Darkie may leave footprints all over it, so I had to tie him up all night. However, Kitty's Rat-Tail was not so easy to control but I managed to coerce Kitty into leaving her inside the house all night so that the tar could dry.

Kitty loved that cat, but like all animals, its life came to an end one day. After lunch I saw her bawling her eyes out on the bed. "What's the matter?" I asked her, but she was inconsolable. It took ages before she was able to splutter out what had happened.

She had noticed that her cat had been missing and hadn't come home last night so she went all around the sheds and the house calling out. When she was out the front of our house near the date palms, she noticed a section of grass that had been flattened. She went over there and sure enough there was poor Rat-Tail laying stiff and prostrate on the ground.

"What have you done with her?" I asked, feeling so sorry for Kitty. She was my best friend.

"She's still there."

I knew how to deal with this as I'd had some practise with one of the pups, which had been run over only a few weeks ago. It was an aspect of life that men had to deal with so I went and collected poor Rat-Tail and took her to the shed. I just had to leave Kitty sobbing on the bed as she took the corner of the sheet from time to time to wipe her eyes and blow her nose. I was glad she was on her bed and not mine! By this time, we had been sleeping on the verandah instead of in our tents, as Mum said she'd seen too many snakes and it was safer for the three of us to sleep on the verandah. I wasn't quite sure if snakes could climb up steps and made a mental note to ask Dad as he always knew about these things.

Dad was in the shed when I arrived with Rat-Tail but he had an engine on. With such a loud noise, it allowed me to proceed with the task of making a coffin out of wood that we collected from freight boxes. I was pleased Dad was occupied. I didn't really want him to ask any questions, so I quickly cut wood and nailed pieces together to make a box just big enough to fit Rat-Tail. I had to curl her tail around quite tight to fit her in, but that didn't matter. She looked like she was sleeping. I wasn't going to show Kitty but I was so proud of my wood creation that I couldn't resist. I thought I'd better wait until the morning, so I hid the box in the corner of the shed under a bag. With Dad's engine still going I snuck out of the shed and whistled as I made my way back to the wood heap and began my afternoon domestic chores.

Saturday was to be the day for Rat-Tail's funeral, so when Jack and Kevin arrived, I prepared the sulky for us to ride in. It was always good when our parents were preoccupied with visitors who needed to organise their tennis matches. The casket had been lined with some fabric Kitty had found and she and Hazel had drawn some pictures to glue to the sides. This was a total secret and Hazel was pleased that she had been included into kid's games, now that she was older. A problem soon arose, however, when we realised that there wasn't enough room in the sulky for five kids, some digging equipment and a coffin.

"Why do we need the sulky, Laurie? Surely we can just walk a little way and dig a hole." I knew Kitty would want Rat-Tail to go to Heaven, so I had the perfect solution, which I had only shared with Jack and Kevin. I didn't dare let on to the girls for fear they would reveal the plan to Mum and Dad. Hazel particularly had yet to learn, that it was not wise to tell our parents everything.

"We're going to ensure that Rat-Tail has every chance of going to Heaven by burying her in consecrated grounds."

This was an expression I'd heard Mum use and I figured that a cemetery was consecrated ground. Dad and my uncles had attended a funeral some time ago at the Winchester Cemetery, which was just east of our school, so I thought that animals could also be buried there. I hadn't told anyone that I was thinking of this for Rat-Tail but, when I told Kevin and Jack at school, they thought it was a good idea. I wished I had thought of it for the pup but I hadn't – instead I had to dig a hole near the dam.

We decided that Jack and Kevin would ride their bikes and I

would take my sisters in the sulky to the Winchester Cemetery. While I harnessed the horse, Kitty made some sandwiches for a picnic, which wasn't entirely a lie. Hazel's job was to ensure Rat-Tail had a smooth ride so she nursed the coffin all the way along the dusty road, past the school and down to the bottom of the hill. As we jerked over the bumps in the road, the clip-clopping of horse's hooves set up a regular sound which offset the discomfort of the heat and sun in our faces.

"Pass over the rake and stones now, Kevin," I panted as I finished digging the hole. We had decided to make a grave in the furthest part of the cemetery near a bare patch of ground. We were mindful that we didn't want anyone to discover our cat's grave but we weren't sure why it might be interpreted as a misdemeanour. Hazel nursed the coffin, with the utmost of importance, while Kitty said a prayer. The flies were buzzing and crawling all over us. I was very pleased that poor Rat-Tail was going to be placed in a hole and covered, away from all the creepy crawlies.

The ride home was tedious, and my tummy rumbled as sweat ran down my back. Slowly I drank from the water-bag as I held the horse's reins, and listened to the hooves on the hard road while I tried hard to ignore the sound of crows. When we were half way home Kitty unwrapped the sandwiches and we allowed the dry bread to roll around in our mouths. I wasn't keen on sandwiches in brown paper, but it stopped my tummy rumbles and soon we could see the house just over the railway line so we knew we were nearly home.

I unharnessed the horse and Kitty and Hazel then went for a ride around the shed. The idea was that I would put away all the equipment and then put our hungry horse in the stable with a bale of hay. Of course as soon as I turned my back, Hazel fell off and started crying. This was not part of the plan and I had visions of a broken arm, like the injury I sustained in a riding fall a few years prior.

"There, there, Hazel," but she continued to cry holding her knee. Kitty was most attentive but I felt annoyed. We had gone to a lot of trouble to provide a Christian burial for the cat and now Mum and Dad were sure to find out what we'd been up to.

"Kitty, take her home, can you? And try to make up some story apart from falling off a horse. We all know it's not the horse's fault."

"Of course, Laurie."

I felt my authority grow. She was a real champion that sister of mine. She had a beautiful smile and such a loving nature. We just had to make sure that our little sister turned out as good as the big sister! When I told Kitty that, she just babied Hazel even more. It was no surprise when years later that nurturing nature of Kitty's manifested into a nursing career – and a good one at that! I felt sure that very soon there would be another cat for Kitty to fuss over and hopefully she would forget all about Rat-Tail.

"Come on, you two. Let's race back for a quick hit of tennis before dinner."

Hazel was easily distracted from her aches and pains, and she was quick to run with us. She knew too if she wanted to play big kid's games then she would have to pick up all the balls that were hit outside the court. When she had served her time doing that then Kitty and I would include her as much as we could in a hit up. Over time, I could see she too had an eye for ball sports, and it was lucky sport was easy for her. For all three of us, sport became a passion which was to remain life-long.

Chapter 9

The Beginning of Bulk Handling

One night, as I lay awake, I heard Dad's car humming down the driveway and gradually pull to a stop. He opened the door and rushed in, so I anticipated something important had happened at the bulk handling meeting. It was April in 1935 and Dad talked excitedly to Mum.

"The meeting favoured a positive response to bulk handling. I seconded the motion and everyone at the meeting was in agreeance."

I was thrilled to hear Dad say this as we'd talked it through last harvest as we bagged the wheat from each paddock, and it was really hard work. I'd wanted to employ more men, with the Depression at its peak, but Dad was always careful with money so I had to continue to heave bags of wheat from ground level onto the truck, ready for the siding. Now Dad was talking to Mum about a deputation being formed to go to Perth to lobby the Midland Railway Company, but by the time he talked through all the details I felt the heavy weight of my eyelids fighting to stay open to hear more of Dad's news. Soon the sleep demon took over and my listening ended.

"Gosh, Dad, who was at the meeting?"

"Well, there was … let's put it this way. There is to be a deputation made up of John Bowman, William Pethick, James Forrester, Albert Bateman and George Ferrier who represent different parts of the district. It's a long process, Laurie. Crickey, it could be years in the making. There will be talk of money and proposals put forward. It's only a start so let's worry about this year's crop first."

With the smell of bacon fading and the sun climbing into the sky, it was time to leave the breakfast table and go to the shed. Dad was right. We had this year's crop to put in first. We planted the crop for 1935 and then the crop for 1936 before more progress was made on bulk handling. It was the harvest of 1936 when our big moment arrived.

Our first load of wheat to the bulk handling bin in Carnamah was a new paradigm in farming and I polished the truck ready to go. I was so excited. I asked Mum to wake me up at three o'clock in the morning so that I could be the first truck to unload with an elevator, operated by Lionel Ferguson, instead of unloading individual bags onto a great stack. My back was very excited as it loved the idea of sitting instead of lifting huge weights.

With my brown paper bag of jam sandwiches and my bottle of tea, I set off in the loaded truck for Carnamah wheat bin, headlights beaming in the early morning. My heart raced in anticipation as I had dreamed of this moment since that night when I heard Dad talking excitedly as he described the meeting. I continued to depress the clutch as I went through all the gears finally reaching full speed as I bounced along the road. I was in heaven! This was soon interrupted as, before me in the line-up, was another truck! That couldn't be right! It was only three thirty in the morning and I could not believe that someone else had the same idea as me – and he'd beaten me to it. It was Jim Adams.

My heart sank as I realised that I'd been pipped at the post. I wondered if his mum had made him jam sandwiches too. This was all I could think about as I roused the highest level of social skills I could muster so that my disappointment did not show. I sat there stunned, and tried hard to subdue the lump in my throat. Finally, I turned off my lights and got out of the truck. It was very difficult to make small talk to Jim Adams and concede defeat.

"We don't always get it our way, Son." Dad was so disappointed too. I'm sure I inherited my competitive nature from him and his total understanding was overwhelming for me as I realised that he wanted to be first too. "Oh well, we'll just have to get on with it I guess."

Not a word was spoken for the next few hours as each of us came to terms with the idea of another person beating us.

"Why don't you and Bill go out and shoot a few birds? Something else to think about for a while. Dogs always need feeding."

I left and went to look for Bill. I soon felt my spirits lift as I realised that this was a new era, and no longer would I have to hump all those bags around and suffer an aching back. Soon the heat of summer and the work of lifting would become a distant memory.

"Bill, just imagine when we no longer have to throw all those bags onto the truck." He seemed rather unperturbed but to me I could feel a weight quite literally lift from my shoulders.

The whole family joined in the lunch time conversation about the new bin and even Hazel showed an interest. "Dad is Carnamah the only new style bin in the state?"

"No. There are eight railway sidings between Marchagee and Mingenew. That's really something. Apparently there have been four gangs of men constructing the bins: one gang laying concrete, one cutting timber, a third erecting the bins and the last gang have put in the floors and added the final touches."

Dad turned to Mum and continued. "It's good really when considering all the news we hear on the wireless about the Depression and many men are without work."

I reflected on Dad's comments and was thankful for old Bill and young Bill. I didn't really want strangers coming and working on the farm but sometimes I knew we had a labour shortage. I had become wary of strangers since Alex and his dad had confronted us in the comfort of our own shed years ago and it stayed with me as a memory for survival, or at least for my comfort. "Dad, let's get out of here. We've got work to do." That was our signal for lunch to finish and shed stuff to begin.

There was much ado in the community about the new bulk handling revolution with an official opening of this 200,000 bushel capacity bin, the largest in the state. John Bowman was credited as being responsible for the installation of the bin and James Forrester, as chairman of the Carnamah District Road Board, officiated at the formalities. There were fun moments associated with it too, as the construction gangs gave a free community concert for two hundred and thirty people. It was a good reason to celebrate with music and dancing and, at the height of the Depression, people looked for opportunities to enjoy life. As a youth, I loved it all, especially when Kevin, Jack and Jim joined in too. There were always lots of kids around and fun was in abundance.

"Well, I tell you what, Laurie. I don't think anyone else will beat us when we create the first bowling green in the area. You wait and see."

Yes, Dad was back in form again, with a new project, an innovator in his field. At moments like that, I so wanted to be like my dad!

Chapter 10

The Search in Belgium

"Dad, wake up. It's time for afternoon tea. We've got to get this bowling green started." I could see he held a letter in his hand, so I took it, headed for the house and left Dad to snooze in the coolness of the truck that was parked just outside the shed.

When I told Mum about Dad and the letter, she took it from me, and her eyes glazed over.

"After the war your father went to look for his brother who had been listed as killed in action. He went by boat to Belgium and began his search for your Uncle Percy. You can read his last letter if you like."

> France
> Sept 17, 1917
> Dear old Howard,
> Your very welcome letter of 7th July arrived a few days ago.
> You will know long before this arrives that I have had my few days leave to England and had a right royal time, had plenty of money although I could not cash that 10 pound money order that you sent. The counter jumper told me that they would have to cable back to Aus to make sure that it was alright and I was not going to wait in London for that so it is not cashed out. I had 10 pound left over beside that so you see it did not matter at all.
> You are shaking things up aren't you with another "Big E". You will not be long with the harvest now. I hope that I will be home for the harvest after this one coming.

I received a parcel from Uncle Arch recently and will drop him a line when convenient to thank him and let him know that I have received it. It will probably be sometime later this week.

The weather here has been beautiful lately but the beauty is forgotten due to the heavy fighting that we have been involved in recently. We are having a little rest from it now for a few days and then I guess it will be on again.

I saw Ralph Deed today for a few minutes. He is looking pretty well. I have not seen any of the other Bamawn Boys but I believe Tom Glover has been killed – 24/3/17.

You do not tell me much country news lately, and by the way, no one told me that Clara was going to Mildura and I believe she went about 24th March. I received her letter last night so I will answer it soon so I don't lose it, but now that I have looked through it there is not much to answer.

How did the Bamawn sport turn out go? Any good?

Well Howard this is about all there is to tell you this trip as things go on the same so I will say good bye for the present with best love to all of you,

From your loving brother,
Percy

In 1919 at the age of twenty-two Dad arrived in Belgium after enduring weeks of sea sickness and exhaustion but this exhaustion was minimal compared to what he endured in the search for his brother, who he could not believe was dead, 'Killed in Action.' It was easy for those army blokes to make a mistake and Dad was determined to seek out these fields near Ypres. With no idea of how to get to Ypres, Dad walked up and down the railway station and looked at every young man he saw. Finally, he spoke to a forlorn looking fellow but he didn't understand what Dad had said. He continued this process, not realising that the population there didn't speak English. His first night in a foreign country was spent sleeping on hard concrete in a dilapidated railway station. He wasn't the only one doing this, much to his surprise.

The next morning he worked out the names of places on a map and proceeded to wait for a train. Towards the end of the day a train stopped but he couldn't pay for his ticket with his Australian currency. This didn't prove to be much of a problem because the ticket collector couldn't care less and told him to find a place somewhere. He found himself amongst the saddest and most ragged looking people he'd ever seen. He looked at every place the train stopped and finally he disembarked at Ypres. He was astounded by the piles of derelict buildings and the poor state of the roads. Indeed, everything seemed to be broken and in a state of disrepair.

Even the people, who wandered aimlessly, were in a daze. Lost souls lingered among the ruins that went on endlessly. He tried to make conversation with anyone but the language barrier limited this. He felt a lump swell in his throat as he realised what he had undertaken after a boat trip halfway around the world. He had arrived at a place where no-one understood him and even his money was no use to him. No-one made eye contact with anyone else, people were very thin and alone and there didn't seem to be a building that wasn't war damaged. The air smelt like rotting garbage and everything was as grey as the weather. It was windy and cold, and somewhere he could hear crying. He was astounded to see that it wasn't a child but an old woman who sat on the side of the road wringing her hands and then wiping them on her dirty, torn apron.

As the woman's dirty hair blew around her face, Dad was shocked to see her poverty through her lack of shoes, despite the stones and potholes on the road. He had some clothes in his case so he offered her a coat. She looked at him in surprise and accepted his generous offer and then garbled something to him that Dad could only assume was trying to thank him.

So, this was the place that his brother Percy had last known.

Dad slept hungry, cold and exhausted. He spent days wandering around, just like everyone else, who seemed to be looking for something, but didn't know what. Occasionally someone would speak English and Dad would engage in conversation with excitement, but they weren't really interested in foreigners, even if this foreigner was a friendly one. An undetermined length of time passed for Dad and eventually some little children took him to their shelter where some adults gave him stale food. The derelict building was a respite and home for this extended family. Only a few could speak English but Dad felt as though all his prayers had been answered.

When Dad explained that he had come to look for his brother, the old man was aghast. "No-one survived here, my good sir. Just look around you. See that mud? Your brother is probably six foot under it. The Jerries slaughtered them all. Those who weren't killed, died of wounds or slid into the mud and died. This place turns into mud in winter and you're lucky now the weather is reasonable. If he was killed in action, he was probably one of the fortunate ones. Others were put in prison camps and starved to death. When did you receive your last letter from him?"

Dad broke down and the tears slid down his face. His limbs felt weak and he had to work hard to control his bodily functions. He couldn't talk and he allowed himself to sink to the ground. The man was patient with him. He'd seen a lot of this since the war ended, that's if wars do ever end. This poor fellow had his own war going on now. Dad blubbered and finally spoke. "He wrote his last letter on September 17th, 1917 from France. The records say he was killed in Belgium on 20th October 1917."

"My good fellow, I can only tell you that he probably didn't suffer too much. You can keep wandering around here looking for ghosts, just like all those you saw in the fields and streets, but I suggest you go home and find some peace. Usually the War Office is pretty accurate. Why don't I take you to Antwerp and put you on a boat for Australia?"

The wave of homesickness that swept over Dad made him weep even more. He heard the man, whose name he didn't know, speak to a young girl. Soon some thin but warm soup was spooned into his mouth.

The boat trip home to Australia was full of nausea and vomiting and Dad thought it was the movement of the angry ocean below the heaving mass of metal. The ship wasn't comfortable, but Dad didn't care. No-one cared. The only noise came from nature in the form of wind or rain and hardly a soul spoke. After a few weeks, Dad began to think about home and wondered how he was going to tell his family about his failure to find his brother.

When Dad arrived at the dock in Melbourne, the sight of his family made him break down again. He was inconsolable, and no-one asked him any questions. When he arrived home to Penrose Farm, his sister Clara helped him out of the car and into the house. Silence prevailed, and it was a blessing when sleep overtook his body. Months later he recovered but his nightmares never left him, and he wondered how on earth returning soldiers quelled their demons in the dead of night.

In 1920 Dad and Mum were married. Uncle Percy's farming property, which was bequeathed to Dad, was settled and life gradually resumed normality in their home at Lockington, near Rochester. Mum was a good artist and Dad was glad that she'd always kept her self-portrait. As a wife and mother Mum was much loved by all her family and she and Dad enjoyed a good life with us. But Dad never fully recovered from the death and the unfulfilled life of our Uncle Percy.

Chapter 11

Fast forward 100 years

Rochester Times

October 20, 2017 In Lockington, Victoria, over 100 family members of Joseph Hector Percy Chappel gathered to commemorate the centenary of his death in World War One. It was on this date, exactly 100 year ago, at 12.30 pm, that Percy was killed, along with two others, as they were bringing up ammunition to the front line in Belgium. The men were seeking shelter from shelling in a dugout. He was hit just over the heart by a piece of shrapnel and died instantly. The three men were buried together, the following Sunday.

The late Percy Chappel had five siblings and each family of these five siblings had been invited to lunch at the Lockington Heritage Complex. Afterwards, speeches by different members of the family followed. Stewart Wallace, the great grandnephew of Percy, presented a powerpoint presentation to outline Percy's last days. This gave the family solace as they now had a chance to say goodbye to a life that was shortened by duty.

Stewart's book, *In the Line of Fire*, reproduces letters and diary entries that Percy wrote in his time at war. No doubt this has been a comfort, though belated, to the family. A copy of the book has been placed at Percy's grave in Belgium when Stewart located the gravesite earlier in the year. A waterproof cover, that Stewart put on, gives the book protection from the weather.

One family member read out a letter that had been published by the local newspaper, and reproduced in Stewart's book. It went like this:

"Mr and Mrs Helmore of Panncobamawn, have received the following tragic letter from their son Pte Fred Helmore. It was written "somewhere in France" under the date 1-11-1917. "The month is going fast and I must get on with my writing. It's been the saddest month of all my army career, for the boy who was my best friend in the forces, has been taken home to be with his god. Of course, you will all know of this, for the sad news of this death will have been cabled through to his father Mr Chappel. On Saturday last, 20th October, Percy and his mates were taking ammunition up to the guns when he was hit over the heart by a piece of shell, and he died instantly. He was buried on Sunday, and not till that night, did I know of his death. It was a big shock to me, for I was with him for an hour on Thursday night, and as we gripped hands and said good-night, little did I know that it would be the last time on Earth that I would see him. We had arranged to go out on Sunday afternoon to buy some postcards to send home for Christmas, but of course, the boy never came down and, in the evening, I heard the news. We were the closest of friends, Perc and I, and though we didn't meet very often, we were always anxious as to each other's welfare. God, it is hard to lose such men as he! He was loved by all his mates. He was brave and willing. Now they realise what they have lost. We are erecting a cross over his grave and I will write to his parents. Well, my dear ones, this is a sad letter to send you, but we must face the reality of things. One thing I find consolation in is that the boy who has gone is far better off than the men who are still fighting for their existence. War and its awfulness trouble him no more. Of course, he had a worse job than we trench mortal men who have no horses to attend to. You cannot imagine what a curse horses are to men in the winter when the poor devils must be fed and tended to in all kinds of weather, wet or dry. Often, at times, there is mud up to their neck. I ask you not to worry, dears, for soon we'll be through with this job. We are making the best of things over here. Just now we are out of action and in good billets and very comfortable, though outside rain and mud are very much in evidence.

Good-night to all."

The entire Chappel family proceeded to the War Memorial where flowers were laid, and quiet time was observed. Later people drove around to look at the family farms in the area. The next day, at church, the Plaque of Remembrance was handed from the West Australia branch of Howard's family to the present-day family members in Lockington. It will be kept in Percy's church.

The photo on the previous page, taken by Sandie Wallace, Stewart's mother, shows Howard's grandchildren who were at Lockington to commemorate the centennial of Percy's death.

A highlight of the day was the presence of the family car that had been sold, but then bought back again, one hundred years later, and restored by the Chappels. Family members could be seen riding around and having fun long into Saturday night!

Clearly, new friends were made and old acquaintances restored at this family reunion and, when the sun set on Sunday night of that weekend, a fitting memorial had been posted for Percy Chappel one hundred years after his death."

Chapter 12

A Bowling Green

We began the construction of our bowling green next to our tennis court. This time we worked during the cooler months of August and September in 1938. It was almost as if we knew that 'extras' needed to be done during non-harvest and non-seeding times. Once again young Bill and I did most of the work as, by this time, old Bill had ordained himself as the shepherd. This  suited his quiet, patient nature. Dad was overseer, but we were quite happy that he left us to our own devices without breathing down our necks. He could be a bit scarey when things didn't go his way.

"Laurie, we need to construct two rinks and when we have a cuppa, I'll tell you why."

I was pleased that Dad shared ideas with me because, in recent times, I could tell something troubled him. I wasn't convinced that it was all about his brother: it happened so long ago.

As I walked along the verandah, I heard Dad talking with Mum so I decided to just listen and not interrupt. "This is pretty major stuff, Bess. Two bowling rinks to be called Marathon Bowling Club. At the meeting, it was decided to limit the number to sixteen members so we'll go with all those present and that'll constitute the foundation members."

"Who was at the meeting, Dad?" I asked casually as I sat down near the scones and jam.

"Mr Fels, Mr Mulligan, Mr Clark, Mr Fogg, Mr Solling, Mr Bentley, Mr Haig, Mr Gell, Mr Cowderoy and Mr Bierman," replied Dad, reading from his piece of paper. "And of course me. That makes eleven and we decided to have the remaining vacancies filled on application and on ballot."

"Crikey, Dad, that sounds pretty selective. But I think that's a grand idea. Serious sport competition is what we want."

"It's not that so much, as being affiliated with the West Australian Bowling Association. The annual subscription will be two guineas plus a night fee for night play. The playing period will be Thursday and Saturday afternoon and evening. We'll also play on Sunday morning but I'm not sure Sunday morning will be a goer. It will clash with Church. Never mind, we'll see how it all works out."

"That's amazing, Dad!"

"Yes, so you'd better make sure that it's all watered and in perfect playing condition."

Over one morning tea my work load had tripled! We had a great water supply as a sand ridge ran through the property just south of the shed and there was a low lying area which was a swamp. It always ensured plenty of fresh water so we were very lucky. Now I had to create a pipe line from the soak to the bowling rink and ensure the windmill was in top working order all the time. We couldn't afford a breakdown now that we had affiliated with the Western Australian Bowling Association, whatever that was. Actually, I didn't want to incur Dad's wrath. I was less anxious to please him now but that didn't abate my desire to do the right thing.

"Bill, we're off gun patrol and birds now. We're full time doing water supply."

I couldn't be bothered explaining it all to him; it was enough to know that the windmill definitely needed to be kept pumping water to that bowling green. I wasn't quite sure if it meant less water for our vegetables and garden but I figured, now I was older, Dad didn't need to concern himself with such trivialities. I certainly got the idea the bowling green was a priority. As for night bowls, that was certainly stepping it up a notch or two. I needed to ensure the diesel supply was kept up for the 32 volt lighting plant and in the back of my mind I heard the engine running twenty-four hours a day. Night bowls? I wondered what Dad was thinking.

I lay in bed that night, still on the verandah, and listened to conversations that drifted from the kitchen table. I was curious and intent on not allowing the sleep monster to have its way so I sat up in the dark, even though my back ached after a while. I clearly heard the clicking of the windmill working methodically so that was good.

"Prices are not good, Bess. This Depression has reached here too and I believe that the bowling green will be a great diversion for people. Wives can come after we have played bowls, for a casserole tea and then sing with the pianola. I knew the pianola was a marvelous thing to have. After some sport, dinner and singing, both men and women will think less about what they hear on the wireless."

As I snuggled down in the comfort of the sheets, I worried about whether or not I should ask someone about the wireless and what they had heard. Should I ask Mum or Dad? What about the tennis court? What about the tennis at Winchester?

I was due to play the tennis singles championships on Sunday at Winchester and it turned out to be a terribly hot day. It had taken me ages to do all my jobs, put fuel in the vehicles and get prepared for the play-off at two o'clock. Even Mum was slow that day as she made my cake for afternoon tea and ensured my clothes were beautifully ironed. I couldn't get my BSA – my old faithful motor bike – started straight away and soon it had flooded so I had to wait a while. I cleaned the carburetta in my spotless tennis whites while trying to stay clean. After a couple of backfires, it finally kicked into life and in the process I'd hurt my ankle. I hoped it wasn't going to interfere with my game. Of course they were all waiting when I arrived but that didn't worry me. Since the time that Jim Adams beat me to the wheat bin at three o'clock in the morning I did things a bit more nonchanlantly. I still couldn't believe he'd arrived before me.

It was almost three o'clock when I finally arrived at tennis and the other players were frantic. "Laurie, we thought you'd have to forfiet to Keith Pethick. He's been warming up since just after midday."

"He's probably nearly worn himself out. Let's get going."

So the match began. I wasn't quite sure what all the commotion was at the outset but a cool breeze came in soon after we started and I quickly got into the rhythm of the game I loved so much. I wished Kitty was there to watch me win the club singles titles and quash any concerns about my lateness. I knew she too would have wondered what all the concern was about. She knew that even if I was late, no matter how late, I would always turn up totally unperturbed. Mum and Dad arrived later, with Hazel, who we had nicknamed the 'kid', but it was Kitty who I missed most as my tennis practise partner.

She was away at Methodist Ladies' College at this stage and I missed her. In later years, when she went on to become a nurse, I felt really pleased for her. I knew Mum and Dad were proud of her and one day when poor Hazel was being reprimanded, I heard Mum tell Hazel she needed to be more like Kit. I wasn't quite sure what that meant but I made a mental note to try and be more inclusive of Hazel in our future activities. With a ten year age gap, it was very difficult but I listened to her when she spoke and gave her opportunities to talk at the table. Previously the table talk had been dominated by 'men's talk', which I thought was natural.

I decided to ask Hazel to listen to the wireless and phone conversations if anyone rang. This was big brother caring I told myself but I was really curious to know what was happening on the wireless so that Dad felt the need to construct not one, but two bowling greens. Of course Hazel blurted it out at tea time and Mum and Dad wondered what on earth was going on. I was a bit embarrassed to have to explain my game-plan. I gave the kid the most evil look I could muster. Little sisters just couldn't be trusted.

The next day in the shed I seized the opportunity to ask about a world espoused by a voice on the wireless. I simply asked old Dave. "What's happening in the world, Dave?"

Dad had employed Dave long ago and part of his role was bag mender which entailed sewing up holes in wheat bags and ensuring they were washed and ready for re-use.

"Remember when I first came to work here, Laurie? Well, there were lots of men looking for work and this farm was on a main road so I thought I had to be really good to make myself employable. I had a wife to keep so I needed a house or a tent or simply something. I was quite happy sewing up holes in bags. Remember the mice plague? Those mice chewing away throughout harvest kept me in a job. But now we have bulk handling of the wheat so the need for bags is lessened. We still need bags without holes for the superphosphate to be delivered by rail. Actually, we need it for the seed wheat too."

"Why were you so desperate, Dave?"

"Lots of men were out of work due to the Depression world wide. Apparently it started in America with the stock market crash, so they tell me, and prices of everything plummetted. This meant many blokes lost their jobs as productivity fell. This has spread to here. You would have heard your father despair over low comodity prices? Well, that means he gets paid less for his grain."

"I didn't realise we were all poor."

"Well, things are tight. People could easily starve. I was really grateful to get a job on a farm and I will do anything to keep it. Your father may even have to reduce my wage but I don't care. See the hut up there that old Bill and I built? That's my home with my wife and my security. See those sheep? That's dinner for all of us here, including Ted here. See those vegetables? Laurie, we won't starve but around the world some people will."

I was stunned. "How is this going to end up?"

"No-one knows, but I'll bet that's what you're hearing on the wireless. There is general uncertainty and then fear often follows. Have you heard of global tensions? It's just another phrase for countries that are fearful. Sometimes this is a reason to worry but, young Laurie, there is nothing you can do about it."

With that, Dad walked in and our conversation stopped. "Dave, you can help Laurie here maintain the bowling green. You can use your initiative regarding what that may entail. And Ted, we need a new tank. Laurie will tell you why." Then he walked out and drove away in the ute. I felt a little bit over whelmed and my head spun with my newly acquired knowledge about the lurking poverty, which we might find outselves in, that could pop up any moment. My sense of authority quickly kicked into action and soon Dave, Ted and I discussed how this bowling green could not only emerge, but thrive. My reputation depended on it so I was excited.

Chapter 13

An Adult World

"Mum, I couldn't sleep last night. I was so worried" I said at breakfast one summer morning in 1938.

"Welcome to an adult world, Laurie, but it's not like you to lose sleep over anything. You're seventeen now so I'm not surprised you would worry about something. Is it Dad?"

"No. I'm just concerned about where the Depression will lead us."

"Oh my! That's profound. It's outside your control so that's not for you to concern yourself with. I'd be more worried about what Dad's going to say if you don't get down to the shed soon to ensure Ted and Dave tend to the bowling green. It's Thursday so people are playing this afternoon and this evening."

With that, I leapt from my seat, grabbed another piece of toast and hurried out of the doorway, letting the fly-wire door bang behind me in my haste. I must try and be a bit nicer to Hazel too. She didn't like being called 'the kid'. She was sitting at the table ready for school. She was such a pretty little girl with a kind nature; in fact, she was very easy to love, and I was pleased she liked school.

Dave got up off his square kerosene tin, which was his seat, and started walking towards me when he saw me coming. "Windmill's working like a charm. It's grass cutting and rolling today and then watering tomorrow." Clearly Dave had the bowling green worked out with mowing and watering on one day and then rolling was to happen the following day. I made a mental note to check the diesel for the lighting plant to ensure the lights stayed on until eight o'clock or so. Ted had completed his work constructing a second tank and now he assumed the role of water and tank man. The water from the soak was pumped into an adjacent tank, then it flowed down to the new tank just near the bowling green to ensure a continuous supply of water ran from hoses and flooded the grass rinks in twenty minute timeslots.

Dave took his empty kerosene can to a shady spot near the tank and appeared to enjoy the tedious work of changing hoses all day long. He must have enjoyed the weekend when bowls were played so the lawn was not watered but I was not going to ask him if he got sick of it. I remembered how grateful they both were to be employed. It was quite incredible how farm tasks just evolved.

The two men were also in charge of butchering every few weeks or so. We all used about the same amount of meat, so they just told us when to have our fridges empty. They then waited for a cool evening to allow the meat to set and the next morning, before morning tea, the cutting up began. Dad usually made himself scarce for that job and somehow needed to go into town for something or he had to go and see someone about something. It was his usual occupation. I, somehow, seemed to be the person the working men consulted, and it was something I felt very comfortable with. While the butchering and meat cutting happened, Mum often used this opportunity to prepare her melon jam in the wash-house, which was an attachment to the house, near the verandah. Melon and pineapple jam was my favourite and I loved it, especially on the scones, when Mum made cream with the separator using our fresh milk.

"Laurie, how should this piece be cut?"

I looked at the butchering book which Dad had bought, but it wasn't clear where all the cutting should happen.

"Dave, let's cut it into quarters and then we can study the picture after. Mum, can you work out where we should cut?"

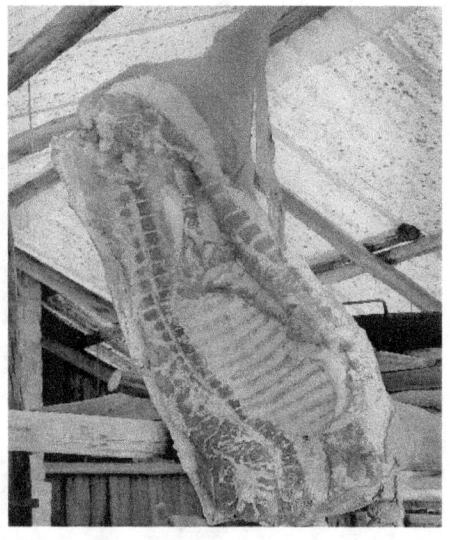

Mum hated the idea of butchering, so she told me to work it out myself and just leave her out in the wash-house doing her jam.

"Any ideas, Ted?"

He didn't know either so we all just trusted each other and worked together to put the meat into the fridge as soon as we could. A big roast always happened the night after butchering and it kept each family in cold meat for the week. The next week another roast was cooked and then the rest of the meat lasted about a fortnight before going slimy. After that the dogs were well-fed and their diet changed from birds and feathers to something they found very attractive. It was easier to keep the meat in winter; in summer, the heat was a challenge but lots of meat was used in sandwiches for paddock lunches when the harvest started.

Dad always operated the harvester; old Bill drove the tractor and I drove the truck into town to deliver the wheat. I had the cleanest job. The others were very dusty. Now that I had officially obtained a driver's licence at the age of seventeen, Dad reminded me that I had more responsibility. I had been driving around the place for years but now I had a piece of paper so I guess that made me a better driver, but I could not quite see the logic. I liked driving the truck during harvest time. It allowed me to talk to others at the bin and organise my social life. It was easier to talk at the bin than use the phone in the house with everyone else listening, particularly Hazel. She kept asking questions that I didn't want to answer. At the bin, there were great opportunities to hear news and arrange tennis matches on a Sunday. On other days, we were too busy harvesting and trying to cart wheat to the bin in case of storms or fires.

Every night at the dinner table I was able to relate a story I had heard at the bin. "Where was the smoke today, Laurie? I saw it coming from Billeroo way."

"No, Mum. It was coming from the south-east past Waddy Forest. It could have been at McGilp's place. Do you remember how they had a fire last year? They say it was started by a log in the copper fire. Someone didn't chop the wood small enough and a great log was sticking out. Of course, it's going to set the place alight eventually and naturally the whole house is going to burn down. Just imagine if that happened again. Surely not! Anyway, someone will tell me tomorrow."

"Bess, you'd better make sure you chop the wood small enough and never leave anything out of the copper fire even if it is on a concrete floor. I know you wouldn't do anything like that. House fires are usually started by kerosene fridges … a bit of soot gets away and whoosh. Up it goes. But truly, how would anyone know how it starts. Now, Hazel, what did you get up to today at school?"

"Well, I rode my bike and delivered milk to the Rhodes's front gate on my way, without any milk spilling. I even remembered to pick up the empty billy."

"Well it's no use crying over spilt milk."

I instantly regretted my corny joke at poor Hazel's expense. Mum and Dad were not impressed either. I had a temporary lapse in judgement, so I had to improve because I had promised myself to be nicer to Hazel. I was going to a dance on Saturday night, so I had to practise being civil. I could not believe I had said something so stupid.

I washed the dishes that night in an attempt to redeem myself while Mum and Dad listened to the wireless. I tried to ask Hazel if she was interested in wiping the dishes, in my effort to be inclusive, but clearly, she was in a huff and refused. She still slept inside so I asked her if she would like a story to be read to her before I went to my tent. I was pleased that she accepted and then I felt forgiven. As I retreated to my tent sometime later, I reflected on the whole idea of sleeping in a tent, when clearly there was room inside the house. I liked being outside and this tent business had just continued since our days at the Ugly Place, long before Hazel was even born.

Chapter 14

Young Bill and Old Bill

It was May of 1939 and the lambs were due to be born so old Bill was very excited. Since assuming the role of Shepherd, he'd become more active and we could see that he grew more involved in the farm. "It's good to see him taking ownership of an important task and, Laurie, everyone needs to feel important. But I'm a bit worried about young Bill. Do you think you could talk to him just to see if he's all right?"

Of course, it was then my role to seek out young Bill and often he was at the shed, but his appearances had become irregular. Even when we went to school, there were many days that he just did not attend and no-one seemed to care. I, on the other hand, never missed a day and the reasons were two-fold. Firstly, Mum always made me and secondly, I liked the company of other kids. I knew too that it was important to learn how to read, write and work with numbers.

"Bill, is everything okay?" I asked when we went on our next bird shooting round. He put his rifle down and walked away so all I could do was wait for him to return, but clearly, I was at a loss to know what worried him. After a few minutes he returned visibly upset and then began to speak.

"My mum's not well. I feed her every night, but she has a dreadful cough and now sleeps all day. I don't want her to die."

Our family spoke about it at the dinner table that night and I waited until Mum put the pie in the centre of the table before I verbalised my real concern. "Mum, what can I do to help him?" She continued looking at her plate for considerable time and then she looked me in the eye.

"Well, Laurie, it could be that Mrs Cornish is going to die. I believe that you will need to wait until young Bill asks for help. Aboriginal people are extremely private and we need to respect their feelings. Oh, I don't know! Perhaps you could ask if there was anything you could do to help. This is never easy."

The next evening, when we were shooting, I asked young Bill if I could help in any way. I was surprised when he asked if I would like to visit her to say goodbye. We got on our motor bikes and took off in the direction of the Ugly Place. It was not really very cold but I could see smoke coming from their chimney in the distance. As we approached some Aboriginal people could be seen wandering between several tents that had been erected near young Bill's house. I must have looked surprised and soon young Bill began introducing me to people who he said were family. There was about a dozen people and we went inside. I felt privileged to have been taken into the world of both young Bill and old Bill, and the feeling of connectedness remained with me for life.

Poor Mrs Cornish was sitting, stooped and rugged up, in front of the raging fire and a young girl was trying to spoon some kind of liquid into her mouth. The smoke was thick in the kitchen and the walls were black from an unkept chimney. Mrs Cornish had her eyes closed and her breathing consisted of noisy inhaling and exhaling that was intermittent with dreadful coughing. Dinner preparations had begun and several little kids were in the kitchen with other adults. I spoke a few mumbled words to the thin woman, and I left the room and stood outside, waiting for young Bill. I thanked him for this courtesy and soon took my leave to return home, trying hard not to show my despair and grief.

Dad told me to let old Bill or young Bill know that the Ugly Place could be used to accommodate family if they wanted it. Poor old

Bill, I felt sorry for him too. All kinds of thoughts went through my head that night as I tried to sleep, and I had many questions. When she died, would there be a funeral at the cemetery I wondered? I hoped Rat-Tail's gravesite would remain undiscovered.

The next morning Mum answered all my questions. "Laurie, we need to respect the family. Clearly many Aboriginal people have come to pay their last respects and we need to give them privacy to do whatever they do."

Hazel suddenly blurted out: "I know some Aboriginal language. Listen to this. Jeengo, Moondug means white woman. That's me. Young Bill is Kajjoo or son, and Mrs Cornish is Yannee or mother." We were all astounded.

"How did you know that?" we all asked in unison.

"Young Bill told me while he was fixing my bike tyre."

Mum continued her line about not presuming to know things that only others knew, which puzzled me slightly, but I was impressed with Hazel's comment. I decided to not pursue it any further, and then tried to think of something to do with farming. "Dad let's get ready for seeding."

"Crikey, have you been outside lately, Laurie? It'll be ages before we can move any machinery. Go and have a look."

There was water everywhere, which assured us of a great season. The rain continued to fall all day and the grass was green, which meant old Bill would soon stop giving grain to the sheep each day. Soon after, the rain stopped and old Bill and young Bill returned to the shed. Although I was curious about Mrs Cornish, I refrained from asking any questions, mindful about respect.

It was Hazel who dropped a bombshell, later that afternoon when I offered to give her a ride on my bike after she got home from school. As she jumped up on the bike, she told me that she had seen what happened to Mrs Cornish a few afternoons  ago when she was meant to be fetching wood from the wood heap.

"Well, I thought I could hear something, so I walked towards the noise and many Aboriginal people were standing around. It was awful. I think they were crying. I saw young Bill and old Bill with their hats off and their heads down looking at the ground. I think they buried her near their house because later I saw a mound of dirt."

Of course, Hazel had to blurt it out at the dinner table that night as well, much to my surprise, but Mum in her wise way normalised it. "Of course, they would bury her. That's what happens when people die. If they buried her near their home, that's quite okay. It's respect for her spirit. You can say a prayer for the family tonight."

Once again, I didn't understand Mum, but I knew when to keep my mouth shut, quite unlike Hazel.

Then Mum continued, "Howard, can you please organise the burial of poor Daisy. She hadn't been herself for quite a while now and when I went to milk her this morning the poor thing was as stiff as a board."

I felt sure I would have to organise either Ted or Dave so when Dad looked my way, I nodded.

The year of 1939 turned out to be eventful but in a very unexpected way. We put the crop in, and it shaped up to be a bumper year. I turned eighteen in July and it felt good to know I had come of age. I had waited about ten years to become a man. The news, however, was not so good one Sunday evening after bowls. When we were all gathered around the wireless, listening to a broadcast given by our prime minister, Robert Menzies, he told us that we were at war with Germany. We were all shocked!

"I think we'll cancel singing with the pianola tonight. Perhaps we'll sit around and say a prayer as we respond to this news and face an uncertain future."

The faces were grim that night and their voices were hushed as they quietly left. Even the kids took their lead from their parents and refrained from games that had become associated with the Marathon Bowling Club.

Oh well, at least we had Kitty's homecoming from boarding school to look forward to soon. In typical Kitty fashion, she could turn her hand to anything and during harvest she delivered the lunches to the paddock each day which relieved Mum of this task. I continued to drive the truck. I loved it when she was home and so did Hazel, who was starting to 'shape up' quite well at playing tennis. Of course, my 'old' partner on the court was in fine

form and we loved every opportunity we could find to fine-tune our skills, winning trophies at the Winchester Tennis Club.

Kitty brought home a friend from school one time and I confess that I found her very attractive. I didn't really like girls much as they talked a lot and laughed too loudly. I had also found that one day they were friendly but the next day they were in a bad mood. I was rather puzzled, so I only took a slight interest in her friend. I was more impressed with Kitty's tennis prowess and her many skills on the court. I also liked Kitty's friend's empathy with Hazel and she was prepared to spend hours playing with her and chasing all the balls she hit over the fence. This was something Kitty and I grew tired of very quickly, so we welcomed any reprieve.

Chapter 15

Training for War

It was Sunday 4th August 1940 when I joined the Army at the age of nineteen, and I remained in the armed services for five years. When I enlisted, I was disappointed that I couldn't join the air force, as my limited education excluded me from this branch of the services. My friend, Sandy McGilp, was accepted into the air force so I thought he was fortunate. Others from the area who joined up at the same time were Les Fowler, Reg Norrish and Gordon Leonard. Men such as Dave Bowman, Harry Kau and Bill Bothe had already joined up and were in our unit, which was called a Militia unit. It was named the 25th Light Horse Machine Gun Regiment.

The first night we slept on straw mattresses at Claremont Oval and it was a sleepless night for us all as we faced the uncertainties ahead. The next day we were transferred to Canning Dam where we did three months of training and I soon became accustomed to army life. I enjoyed the company of men and learning new skills. Soon we learnt how to march and how to use the Lee Enfield rifle. The Vickers gun was British-made and was a water-cooled unit, firing point 303 inch bullets at 500 rounds per minute when it was loaded onto a tripod. We had three months of training and then three months of leave.

It was on my three months leave at home when I learnt that the Japanese had declared war on the Allies, so full time training began at Northam Army Camp. Soon I volunteered for overseas service as part of the Australian Imperial Force and I hoped that we would go overseas as a whole unit, but this did not eventuate. Our unit had to defend the homeland and the situation changed very quickly. I was a member of C. Squadron in the 25th L.H.M.G. Regiment. There were three squadrons in this Unit - A, B and C. Our squadron was delegated the task of defending the area south of Fremantle and, with this is mind, we were based at Coogee Beach. We were then moved to Pearce Aerodrome and then back to Northam. We were issued with Bren Gun carriers and I undertook training to become a carrier driver, which involved vigorous training and exams. I topped the class and this gave me something to write about in my letters home as I knew Mum and Dad would be very proud of me. The months of moving around the coast, in a defensive capacity, continued and soon the months had turned into years.

After being constantly moved around between Coogee and Port Gregory we arrived at Northern Gully, to the east of Geraldton, in early June of 1943. By September, a Japanese invasion appeared far less likely so our unit was disbanded. The younger men, like myself, were sent to Sydney and then on to Kapunda in Queensland for jungle training. This training was nothing short of torture and so much harder that being in action, but I survived knowing that, if I went to the northern islands, I had to be prepared. This continued for four or five months but there were often good times as I enjoyed picking all types of fruit and loved being surrounded by big trees with lush foliage. About once a week I had a reprieve as my driver training enabled me to be selected to move military artillery around, so I drove the steep, winding hazardous road between Wondecia, on the Atherton Tablelands, three thousand feet above sea level, and Cairns on the coast.

We soon got word we were going to be sent to New Guinea and there was a sense of excitement with four days leave being granted before we left the mainland of Australia. My friend Tommy Sargent and I went to Innisfail and were shocked at the price of drinks. We had to pay four shillings for a bottle of beer. Nevertheless, we bought beers and enjoyed time away from the base, with the knowledge that our future was uncertain.

As I sat down to write to Mum and Dad, I was deeply aware of Dad's letter from Uncle Percy, written during the last war, that he had kept for so many years. The fact that he had it in his pocket one day at work and read it, was scary. I hoped this wasn't going to happen again for our family. I read through Mum's letter as I took out my paper and pen, so I would have some ideas for a reply. I looked fondly at the photo of Mum and Dad.

My young friend Jim White was working at Marathon and this turned out well. I was pleased. I liked Jim and, as I remembered our marble days at school, I could feel a smile spreading across my face. He was the little kid and I was the big kid. A fairer person one would not meet, and I remembered how much I loved playing sport with him and against him. I felt a lump come into my throat and quickly thought of something else. This was not the time or place for homesickness of any kind to creep in. There was no mention of young Bill or old Bill and I often thought of young Bill's skills, as a marksman, and what a valuable contribution he would have made if he enlisted. I was unsure how he would have handled the training with all its rigor. As I looked through Mum's letter, a photo of Kitty dropped out. She looked amazing. She had finished her training as a nurse and was now training to be a mid-wife. I imagined Mum and Dad's heart, bursting with pride. I was not sure what Hazel was doing but I would remember to ask in my letter.

This turned out to be my last reasonable letter home due to the constant humidity in New Guinea. Any paper was always wet. I knew, however, a mere few lines, no matter how scrappy, was a comfort to those at home. I put the photos in my pocket, wrote my letter home and set off for camp with Tommy.

Chapter 16

Going to War

The boat trip to New Guinea lasted five days and I was unbelievably sea sick. I couldn't think about anything except how dreadful I felt and how much I wanted to get off. There were about 1,000 of us aboard an American ship called the *Thomas Corwise*, and many men were sea sick. Even after we arrived, I was sick for days. I slowly recovered and became accustomed to life in a camp of Americans and Australians in a town called Aitape. The American soldiers had a picture show which we were all able to attend, but it was so hot and humid we found it hard to focus on the film. It rained most days in the late afternoon and soon we found the rain was warm and not the least bit uncomfortable. Being near the coast, we heard the ocean's soothing sound which put me to sleep each night.

After about six weeks, we were told that we were heading to the front line to relieve the Americans who were in contact with the Japanese soldiers in the Finisterre Mountains. This campaign was known as the Aitape Wewak campaign and I will explain the organisation.

There were ten men in each section, three sections in a platoon, three platoons in a company and four companies in a battalion. Then there were three battalions which made up a brigade and three brigades in a division. In total this made approximately a thousand men in a division. I made a mental note to tell Dad in my next letter as I knew he would be interested.

I was in B division of the twenty sixth battalion and an amazing man called Major Dave Hey was our leader. We all had total confidence in him and soon we were issued our combat clothing and kit. While I had an Owen gun and ammunition, others had rifles, and we operated as a company which consisted of ninety men. Our leader gave us order to address all officers by their Christian name only, as opposed to their rank, because we were in the enemy listening zone. If the Japanese could identify officers, they could be targeted.

We set off on the first ten miles by truck and then on foot and had to slash the dense jungle vegetation with our machetes. We marked the end of every mile with a ten-minute break. This continued through native villages until nightfall. We would make a perimeter trench, which always faced outwards, for sleeping in. Daily we pushed on uphill into the Finisterre Mountains. The afternoon rain created mud and slush but brought slight relief from the heat and our exhaustion.

We moved in single file along tracks from one native village to another. We slashed our machetes as we went. We knew that our jungle training in tropical Queensland put us in good stead for this. After five days we saw a skeleton on the side of the track and, on closer examination, we identified the Japanese uniform, so this increased our awareness and our adrenal system worked overtime.

The natives told us that the Japanese were in the next village now. The Americans moved past us and then moved back behind. We relieved them, as planned, so we knew an attack was imminent. We gave the natives food and they gave us information, which suited everyone. Our planned attack was the next morning so our sleep that night was very fearful as we were unsure if we would survive the next day. Our aim was to push the enemy back to Wewak while the rest of the sixth division pushed towards Wewak along the coast.

Gordon Ellis and I were forward scouts, and we took a sentry boy with us. He was a native who knew the jungle, and he was to find out where the enemy was positioned. After he gave us information, he retreated to his village while our men moved into position to form an ambush. We attacked and gave the enemy all the fire power we had. I threw a grenade, which became caught up in some bush, and rolled back towards me. Luckily, it went off without doing any damage. The enemy fired back of course and soon we spotted a Japanese soldier in a foxhole about twenty foot to our right. Gordon was on his hands and knees and I was next to him flat on my stomach. The Japanese soldier fired at us and one bullet grazed Gordon creating a deep scratch. Thankfully the bullet skidded past him and over the top of me. It was lucky I was lying down as I heard it whizz above me. One of our men shot the occupant of the foxhole and we went on to take up our position without further casualties. This was our first experience of action but there was plenty more like that ahead.

After the retreat of the enemy, our trench perimeters were

formed, and we prepared for the night ahead. Suddenly there was a burst of gun fire from a Bren gun, which was covering the perimeter of our trenches to protect us from the enemy. We heard a scuffle and voices. The machine gunner realised he had hit our patrol leader, who had just returned. Our gunner mistook him for a Japanese soldier. The patrol leader died instantly, and the gunner was mortified. We buried our man the next day, knowing it would possibly be six months before the graves unit would come through. We knew by that time the vegetation in the jungle would have grown back over. It was a glum morning and we were all on edge. At this point we were relieved by another company which gave us the chance to regroup and recover from the trauma.

The deeper we penetrated the jungle, the stiffer the opposition became but at the same time we became more experienced. By radio we were able to call the Air Force for a bombing raid to enable us to mark the position. This, along with the three-inch mortar, undoubtedly saved many Allies' lives. The bombers also dropped off our food supply which consisted of Bully Beef and biscuits which tasted like cardboard. We ate this and didn't mind sharing it with the natives of New Guinea, who were later acknowledged as being instrumental in the ultimate Japanese surrender.

Malaria was also a problem we dealt with, so each man had to take one Atabrine tablet each day to stop any symptoms. This became part of our supplies so, with around two thousand men in these Mountains, distribution was a challenge. Daily we depended on food, ammunition and Atabrine tablets. I heard the bombers flying low and when I looked up, I could see the men trying to work out when to push out our life sustaining supplies. We had to ensure we didn't get hit by these flying missiles as the boxes often broke open and tins would be flying everywhere.

A more efficient way to ensure supplies arrived safely was to use the natives who formed a human chain and carried our boxes up the mountains. They slashed through the jungle and sweated profusely as they toiled. They did an outstanding job and we were indebted to them. Their reward was to eat some of the Bully Beef and hard biscuits. In all my time there I never heard anyone complain.

We were always concerned about our casualties and one of our fears was the Woodpecker, a Japanese heavy machine gun. It had a slow rate of firing and fired around sixty rounds per minute. Our Bren guns fired at five hundred rounds a minute and the Owen gun was faster still. The issue with the Woodpecker was it would start firing and continue for about ten minutes. There would be thirty minutes of silence and then it would start again. The enemies aim was high and we heard bullets constantly whistling through the trees. We were unsettled to know they were always so close, both at night and during the day.

One day, when the woodpecker stopped, we were told the bombers were to attack and we would follow up to take command of the position. We went in with all guns blazing only to find the Japanese had abandoned their position but had left the woodpeckers behind. They had been too heavy to carry, and we didn't use them because we had no suitable ammunition. This was how our operations tended to go and we were always mindful of sniper fire. At one stage Jack Cox and I were digging slit trenches around the perimeter in our move forward. Major Dave Hey walked out in front of where Jack and I were working, when suddenly a shot rang out causing Dave Hey to fall to the ground. We took him inside the perimeter and discovered he'd been shot in the lower body. We made him as comfortable as possible and the natives then carried him back to Aitape to hospital, a trip which would have taken eight or nine days. His pain would have been unbearable for the duration of that time. It was distressing but I was thrilled when I heard he had survived. He lost a kidney but went on to be an administrator in New Guinea after the war. I was indebted to this man for saving my life earlier in the campaign as I realised the sniper bullet could well have killed me.

As we progressed forward, we saw the enemy had pushed out the natives from their villages and had taken over their homes and gardens as their own supply line had been cut off. The natives came to us as we fed them and were sympathetic to their homelessness.

We had to keep moving forward and our next Japanese encounter was in a village called Gadnigem and it was here that things became scary. Jim Curly and I were instructed to go back to our previous camp or perimeter position and tell them to come forward. I led the way and soon came across an old tree trunk that was laying across the track. I stopped, put my foot on the trunk and said to Jim, "I think we're on the wrong track." I can't remember what he said but we turned around and we thought the whole Japanese army was shooting at us. There were bullets flying everywhere and we ran for our lives. We were in such a panic that we missed the turn off for Gadnigem and ended up completely lost.

The sun had almost set and we were in Japanese territory; we knew this because of the boot marks – the Japanese boots had round studs on the sole whereas we had square studs. Suddenly there was a Japanese soldier right in front of us. He appeared to be totally unarmed and looked just as surprised as we were. As he turned and ran, Jim raised his rifle and aimed at him.

"No, no," I said. "The sound of the shot will give our position away."

We soon came across a swamp and when the sun set, we waded through the shallow water. I was terrified as I could not see us getting back to our unit in the dark. We would have to wait here until morning. We were in water all night but it had some advantages. We would be able to hear any human noise, so from this perspective we were relatively safe, but I was concerned that our malaria symptoms would return if we couldn't have access to our supplies soon.

After a long night that I thought would never end, the day began to break and soon I heard 'music to our ears'. The mortars were starting up and each mortar had two explosions. The first one was from within our perimeter, so this gave us a sense of direction. With the sun rising I knew it had to be over my right shoulder. Jim did not have a clue, so he just followed me and my directions thankfully. For several hours we pushed through tall, thick swampy grass, with our machetes, listening for the sound of the mortars, which were thankfully sounding closer. We kept the sun over our right shoulders and towards lunchtime we broke through onto a track. We were both so relieved but still had to enter the perimeter without attracting friendly fire. We saw a native boy who was carrying water into the enclosure so we convinced him to tell the others we were back. Soon he returned and took us back into the camp. Everyone was ecstatic! A message had been sent back to Australia to advise our families we were missing but it was quickly stopped before reaching our home places. That night, for my two hours, I slept soundly thankful that the good Lord had been watching over us. Unfortunately, this kind of daily activity continued for years.

Chapter 17

The End is in Sight

The talk around the camp sometime in August 1945 was all about the atomic bomb the Allies had dropped on Hiroshima in Japan and, by all accounts, it had caused a lot of damage, creating seventy thousand casualties.

"Laurie, I've just heard that another bomb has been dropped on Nagasaki, a place in Japan. I guess that would have to be good news."

"Well, my good friend Jim Curly, all I can say is that someone sure has decided to turn up the fire power on those Japs."

Soon the Japanese surrendered but the trouble was the Japanese in New Guinea didn't know the surrender had taken place. It was lucky we didn't lose any more men and soon there was a real buzz around the camp. Our daily adrenaline was still high but it meant we could soon sleep a bit easier at night when we were off duty. Those men on duty were always mindful of snipers in trees, in traps or just around the corner. It was the moment we had been dreaming of for years.

In a matter of days we received orders to clear an area for aircraft to land. With the help of the natives, who by this stage were starting to gain a real understanding of English, we cleared the whole area where there had previously been an air strip. Out of respect for Major Dave Hey, we named the airfield The Heyfield. This became a critical part of our evacuation as we were then transported to Wewak. Without the airstrip, our evacuation would have taken weeks instead of days. We were so happy, at last, and soon realised we could be on our way home, so we enjoyed the physical comfort of Wewak. Gradually a few smiles crept onto men's faces and taunt muscles started to relax.

The next thing was the surrender of the Japanese Forces and we all watched as the arrogant Major General Adachi alighted from the plane and stepped onto the tarmac. He had arrived from somewhere in New Guinea but we didn't care. All we cared about was the finish of our time here. It was too early to contemplate anything else.

There was silence on this hot day and we could all feel the sweat running down our backs as all the important men brought the Adachi Wewak-Campaign to an end. Our unit had been in action for six months. During the campaign our 6th Division lost five hundred and eighty men. It was difficult not to feel a real mixture of emotions, but we all stood there somewhere in the crowd and watched the historical moment. By that stage we were able to control the urge to vomit or faint, but somewhere behind me I heard a rustle and I knew someone just could not help himself and my heart bled for him. We were nearly there, and we had to be strong for just a little while longer, standing to attention in the midday sun, for what seemed to be an eternity. I easily curbed the urge to look around and was fortunate enough to be in the front row so I could see what happened. I focused on the men moving towards the podium. Major General Robertson, who was the commander of the Australian Forces in New Guinea, took the sword from Major General Adachi. It was all over.

I thought about Dave Hey and often wondered if I would ever see him again. Many faces were ingrained in my mind and I will never forget the friendly fire incident so many years ago when we first arrived. We had sweated for years and we all had feelings of relief now. We just wanted to go home.

These was a buzz around the camp after the official business and we were eager to find out how our evacuation was going to happen. It was worked on a point system. The longer you had been in the army, the more points you acquired so those with the most points would be the first to go. I could hardly believe it when my name was called out as I didn't really think I'd been there longer than others. It was unbelievable but I found out later that Dad had applied to the authorities to have me discharged early so I could help with the harvest.

There were about thirty of us who left that day on a Lancaster Bomber. The belly gun had been removed and the hole had been covered with boards which had spaces about half an inch apart. We didn't care how we were going. We were leaving and we were ecstatic. We were told to take a blanket with us as it would be cold, and all our gear was unavailable to us during the flight. We did not care, and no one took a blanket, but soon after take-off the wind started whistling up between the boards. After feeling so hot for years, we couldn't believe how cold it was as the plane continued its ascent over the Stanley Ranges. Of course, as the plane climbed higher, it grew colder and soon we were freezing. Someone called out, "Don't tell me we're all going to freeze to death now." That was exacerbated, too, by the shortage of oxygen which made us breath twice as fast to keep up our air supply.

I looked out the window and saw a sheet of flame coming from the exhaust of the engines and would have given anything to warm my hands up on those flames. There were two engines on each side of the plane so there was plenty of warmth outside but none inside. We were only in our jungle greens and every now and then the door of the pilot's department opened and men in leather jackets would ask us how we were going. Of course, we were not going to complain but I was glad when we arrived in Brisbane and I could hardly believe we were on home soil.

Chapter 18

Marathon – Here I Come

We arrived in Melbourne on Melbourne Cup Day in 1945, traditionally the second Tuesday in November. We were hoping to see the horse race but were taken, as always, to an army camp and this time it was at the Melbourne Show Grounds. By now we were becoming impatient with the discharge procedures as they seemed to take forever. We listened to the wireless that night and learnt that Rainbird won the race. We decided that next year we would place a bet on the Melbourne Cup and would remember this horse race day forever. Our spirits were upbeat, and every plane journey meant we were closer to home. Before we went out that night, I found my photo of my last day at Marathon and this photo allowed my homesickness to abate. Soon I would be there with my family on our farm and now my stomach lurched with excitement for that great reason.

I still had to see my time out in Melbourne. We were all excited at the thought of a meal in the nearest café and my mouth watered at the thought of a huge steak. We all ordered steak and eggs but about half way through we realised we just couldn't eat any more. We were dismayed really as we had dreamed about this moment for so many years. Our stomachs had shrunk as we adapted to army food and limited rations. I could hardly believe it when I had to leave half my meal behind.

Soon I was on the train bound for Western Australia and once again I had to stay at the camp at the Claremont Showgrounds until I was finally discharged. I could not believe the war finished in August and it was now November.

The first thing I did was use my ten-pound army allowance to buy myself a new suit and then I caught the train to Winchester and my home. This was the last part of my journey and I wondered how Kitty and Hazel would have changed. I remembered Mum's cooking and Dad's face and then found a lump had formed in my throat. This time I gave in to the lump and soon tears flowed freely. I was very happy, and I had reason to be, but I was soon to find out how many men from our area didn't survive. All the way home I thought about how change would manifest itself in my life. I was keen to start harvest with Dad and I wondered about dogs that had died and men who may have moved on. By focusing on practical aspects of farming it allowed me to minimise my sentimentality and eventually eradicate that lump.

I wanted to walk home from Winchester Station and walk through the main gates. I looked up at the big gum trees that moved constantly by the wind or birds. I wondered if young Bill was still shooting. Of course, he would be. Dogs always needed feeding. I listened for the sound of the gun and realised I wouldn't need to be fearful any more. The dry heat felt good and my stomach growled for some of Mum's cooking. I couldn't smell anything at that time but as I squeezed my eyes tight to look westwards into the setting sun, I wondered who I would see first. I wondered if someone would be waiting for me?

I heard Jim call out. "Laurie, is that you?"

He ran towards me, all grown up, but I would have recognised him a mile away. I tried to run but my gear was too heavy. I dropped it and ran. I ran towards Marathon – my home I had dreamt of for five years. I felt the lump threaten to come again so I thought of 'man stuff' to talk about with Jim. We were both breathing heavily, but we managed to give each other a huge hug. I didn't want to let go and soon Mum and Dad were there as well.

They had all grown older but the smell emanating from the kitchen was heaven. There were so many gaps to fill in over the five years that no one knew where to start.

"What happened to old Bill? Is young Bill still shooting? I just want to hear it all."

"Old Bill died, Laurie, and we gave him a burial in the Winchester Cemetery. Young Bill joined a group of young fellows in Carnamah and now he is part of a shearing team. Things have changed, Laurie, but that's to be expected. Jim's still winning tennis, aren't you, Jim. Let's play the pianola after dinner and allow you a bit of breathing space. Some music may be good for your soul."

Dad, as always, was right. I felt myself gradually grow tired on my first night home and was soon asleep. But my sleep was full of strange dreams. With Kitty and Hazel grown up and establishing their own lives, I had visions of a new life for myself. I was close by, on a farm with more acres, just like Dad when he came from Victoria.

I was relieved when I woke and normality resumed with Mum's

big breakfast and the kitchen still as I remembered.

I still felt tired, in fact I felt exhausted, when Dad and I walked to the shed.

"Son, your exhaustion is only to be expected. You've been to hell and back. Going to war is totally traumatic and it's going to take some time to recover, but you will. Why don't you have a kip in the truck while I take the tractor into the paddock? Jim and I will manage for a few days. Just take it easy."

I climbed into the truck and slumped along the hard seat. I promptly fell into a deep sleep in the most cramped, uncomfortable position. I woke up with a start as Dad was banging on the truck door.

"Come on. Laurie. It's time for afternoon tea. Your mother has just put the kettle on."

I had never heard such sweet words and felt all the comforts of home. As we walked together towards the house, I thought of saying,

"Dad, it was all about the gun."

However, he talked of farm business and gradually I put guns out of my mind. Instead I consumed myself with life on Marathon, near Winchester, and the year of 1945 gradually drew to a close.

Epilogue

My father Laurie Chappel spent considerable time on Marathon recovering from the war and generally immersing himself in farming and country life. He always enjoyed his sport and socialising afterwards. My brother, Lindsay Chappel, tells the story of accompanying Dad to Marathon many years later to find his motor bike, which he regularly left at the front gate in his youth to avoid alerting his parents to the lateness of his homecoming.

Dad purchased his own farm, Hindmarsh, which consisted of 3000 acres in a nearby area Perenjori. Like his father, he wanted to up stakes and move, increase his acreage and have better opportunities. This was a post war era of sport, country town socialising and Masonic Lodge. It was an era of scant regard for rules whether it was roping two trucks together to transport machinery or simply doing what one had to do to survive. Dad worked hard on the farm but my brother says he only worked as hard as required to be successful and ensuring there was a lot of fun and happiness to go around. I guess this is true and this is what I remember of my father.

It was an era when young men returned from the war eager to embrace life, realising they were lucky to have survived. During this time the Perenjori Roads Board became the Shire of Perenjori. Dad was an  elected member of this organisation for over twenty years and was president for six, so between the Shire and Lodge Dad indulged his love of public speaking. He opened the Perenjori Pioneer Wall and gave his audience a detailed history of farming, and the video has been retained in the Battye Library in Perth

He filmed the 100 year celebration of Morawa which is also in the Battye Library. His own account of survival, during his war experiences, is also kept as a historical document in the Battye Library. He was a legend in town and a hero at home.

He married our mother Audrey Brown at the age of 29 and had two children. He also worked with his father at Marathon for many years and one day the men decided to construct a shed. Dad's father laid the wooden trusses on the ground but thought there wasn't enough pitch on the roof, so he moved the rafters a bit. It turned out that moving the rafters and making up his own rules resulted in a shed that looked like a church. Their belief was that it didn't hurt to have a building that resembled a church on

his farm. Making up rules was normal practice.

Dad was a founding member of Morawa and Perenjori Bowling Clubs. He later became a founding member of the Warwick Bowling Club when he retired to Perth.

In his later years he travelled around Australia in his caravan, on his own, visiting family in Victoria and places of interest. He was away for months at a time, year after year. He never lost his curiosity and zest for life.

He lived to 97 – a life well lived – and died suddenly of a heart attack at home in 2019.

Other books by this author:

A Rough Road

About the Author

Lyn lives in Perth with her husband Greg and enjoys spending time with her children and grandchildren. In her spare time she enjoys travelling, spending time with friends and researching family history. She is currently employed as an educational supervisor for three Perth Universities so this keeps her busy. She retired from teaching several years ago.

www.ingramcontent.com/pod-product-compliance
Lightning Source LLC
Chambersburg PA
CBHW071006080526
44587CB00015B/2360